CAN SQUID FLY

?

Answers to a host of
fascinating questions about the sea and sea life

TONY RICE

This little volume is dedicated to Kris, my 'senior management', soulmate and constant whale-spotting companion with eyes like those of an SH! Thank you for your infinite patience.

Also by Tony Rice: *British Oceanographic Vessels 1800–1950,*
Decommissioning the Brent Spar (with Paula Owen),
Voyages of Discovery,
Deep Ocean,
Do Whales Get the Bends?

Published by Adlard Coles Nautical
an imprint of A & C Black Publishers Ltd
36 Soho Square, London W1D 3QY
www.adlardcoles.com

First edition published 2011

ISBN 978-1-4081-3320-0

A CIP catalogue record for this book is available from the British Library.

This book is produced using paper that is made from wood grown in managed, sustainable forests. It is natural, renewable and recyclable. The logging and manufacturing processes conform to the environmental regulations of the country of origin.

Typeset in Rotis Semisans 10/13.5pt by Palimpsest Book Production,
Falkirk, Stirlingshire.
Printed and bound in Spain by GraphyCems.

Note: while all reasonable care has been taken in the publication of this book, the publisher takes no responsibility for the use of the methods or products described in the book

CONTENTS

WHAT'S IT ALL ABOUT?

In 2010 I published *Do Whales Get the Bends?*, a little book attempting to answer 118 'frequently asked questions' about the oceans, ranging from how big they are to who owns them. It was inspired by my experiences as a lecturer on cruise ships and the sorts of questions that fellow passengers asked me. Many of the answers were based on my own experience as a life-time biological oceanographer, but quite a few of the questions were well outside my area of expertise. Hopefully I admitted as much at the time. Finding adequate answers required a fair amount of research on my part – and I found the process fascinating, because I came across an enormous amount of (to me) new information. This new book tries to do much the same as the first, answering a new raft of questions, many of which stumped me initially.

Like *Do Whales...?*, this book covers a pretty wide range of topics from biology, geology and ocean physics and chemistry, through fishing and fish-farming to navigation and shipping. But this time I've put in quite a bit about organisations of various sorts, prompted by questions like 'Who decides what can and can't be thrown overboard?', 'How many containers can a ship carry?' and 'What on earth does Maersk mean?'. Where I think they are particularly useful I have also included website addresses.

As before, I've tried to deal with the topics in bite-sized pieces that can be read in ten minutes or so. Most of the answers are therefore in the 500–1,000 word range, although a few are a good deal longer. Again, as in *Do Whales...?*, I've used fairly simple and, I hope, clear sketches to illustrate particular points. But this time I've also been able to include a few photographs. These are mostly my own and, since I am by no stretch of the imagination an expert photographer, they will certainly not be the best photos you've ever seen and for cost reasons they have to be in black and white. However, they have one very important redeeming feature. They have been taken by a non-expert (me) from conventional cruise ships and with a fairly ordinary camera and lens[1], so they could easily have been taken by almost anyone. Their significance is therefore what they show you if you know what you are looking at, hopefully explained in the accompanying

---

1 For those of you interested in these things, the camera I use is a now greatly out-of-date Canon EOS 350D with a Sigma 70–300mm lens.

text, rather than illustrating what you might see with extremely complex and expensive equipment operated by a highly skilled technician.

Another fairly minor departure from *Do Whales...?* is that this time I have included a 'Further reading' section, a short list of references you can go to for more detailed information or, sometimes, an alternative view. You will also find most of these references in one or other of the rather large number of footnotes I've added to expand on bits of the answers. I'm a great fan of footnotes from the points of view of both a reader and an author because they provide a refuge for all sorts of odd bits and pieces that the author, at least, thinks are too good to ignore but which might break up the narrative if left in the main text.

Finally, I've written a little introduction to each of the major sections to let you know the reasoning behind what is, and what isn't, in it.

Happy reading!

Tony Rice, August 2010

I

Life in the Oceans

This section, like the following one on Edible Marine Biology, is something of a mixed bag, the only common feature being that the questions deal entirely with living creatures, both plants and animals. *Do Whales...?* included quite a lot on biology, from the tiny plants of the phytoplankton that support almost all marine life, through some of the simple animal groups and the shellfish, to the fish, birds and mammals. Inevitably, lots of interesting questions had to be left out. This one tries to fill in a few of the gaps.

1 How many different creatures live in the oceans?

I tried to answer this question in *Do Whales...?*, pointing out that our view of the biodiversity of the oceans has changed dramatically over the last 150 years or so, and more so than of any other environment on earth. This is because in the middle of the 19th century, although the shallow coastal waters of the earth's seas were known to carry an abundance of different species, almost all the best-informed scientists of the day were convinced that the harsh living conditions of very low temperatures, immense pressures, total darkness and acute shortage of food meant that the deep oceans were totally devoid of life. This turned out to be quite wrong and it was soon discovered that animal life was to be found at bottom of the very deepest parts of the oceans, several kilometres beneath the surface. Nevertheless, for more than a century – until well into the 1960s – the results of many expeditions to sample the animal life in the deep ocean seemed to indicate that life in the deeper parts was pretty sparse and not very varied. In other words, the deep sea was thought to be a very low biodiversity environment.

Things changed very rapidly over the next 20 or 30 years, especially with respect to the communities living actually on or in the sea floor rather than in the water column. By the 1990s most deep-sea biologists believed that, rather than being a low biodiversity world, the deep sea floor might well be the most biodiverse environment on the planet, possibly housing tens of millions of species, most of which have yet to be discovered. Partly as a result of the realisation of just how ignorant we were of this huge environment, the largest habitable one on the planet, moves to try to rectify the situation began in the early 1990s. These culminated in the establishment in 2000 of an international collaborative project, the Census of Marine Life (CoML), now involving scientists from more than 80 nations around the globe (see www.coml.org). The incredibly ambitious objectives of the programme were to produce, in 2010, 'the world's first comprehensive Census of Marine Life – past, present and future'.

This was a tall order indeed, and one that they were bound to fail to achieve. Nevertheless, they have made great strides in the last ten years. Starting from the basis of an estimated 230,000 different marine animal species having been described and with specimens preserved in the world's museums, CoML partners have added well over 5,000 new species over the past decade, with many more to come within the next few years. These numbers don't even start to scratch the surface of the estimated huge marine biodiversity among multicellular animals still to be uncovered. But a spin-off from CoML, the International Census of Marine Microbes or IcoMM (see http://icomm.mbl.edu/), is coming up with some awe-inspiring numbers. When IcoMM kicked off in 2003, microbiologists had identified about 6,000 different kinds of marine microbes and predicted that there might actually be something like ten times as many, that is about 600,000. How wrong they were. After sampling at more than 1,200 different localities around the world, IcoMM researchers found hundreds of thousands of different microbes and compiled a database of 18 million different DNA sequences. Not all of these sequences necessarily represent separate species, but the experts involved now estimate that there are at least 20 million different kinds of microbes in the ocean – and possibly billions or even trillions.

My mind starts to turn cartwheels when confronted with these sorts of numbers. But in for a penny, in for a pound, as they say. How about this for another mind-bending piece of nerdish maritime information? By many standards, our tiny planet is just a speck of dust compared with the vastness of the universe as a whole. Nevertheless, it is pretty unusual in being one of the relatively rare specks that have acquired this amazing phenomenon we call life – most of it, of course, in the oceans. Now here is the gobsmacking statistic. A reasonably confident estimate of the total number of individual microbes in the oceans is 10^{29}, a number that I can't even begin to imagine. And no wonder, because it turns out to be 10 million times the estimated total number of stars in the universe. Try that out on the grandchildren!

2 Why do animals and plants have unpronounceable Latin names?

In *Do Whales...?*, I used quite a lot of scientific Latin names for various marine creatures, in some cases because they don't have ordinary or common names. This prompted a number of questions about the naming of animals and plants and why scientists often seem to make them unnecessarily complicated. This is my attempt at an answer.

Basically, it's all down to an 18th-century Swedish naturalist and physician called Carl Linnaeus. Linnaeus was born in 1707 at Råshult, a village in southern Sweden, where his dad was the local priest. The young Linnaeus studied medicine at the University of Lund and then in Holland and eventually became professor of medicine at the University of Uppsala, a post that he occupied until his death in 1778. However, his main interest was in natural history and particularly in botany, which at that time was central to any medical education. He made a number of plant-collecting trips around northern Europe and received plants from various other parts of the world, mainly from his ex-students. Plant classification at that time was pretty chaotic and Linnaeus' first major scientific contribution was a new system of classification based on the reproductive organs of flowering plants. This Linnaean system has long since been superseded, but his other main contribution, the so-called binomial system, still dominates the naming system in both botany and zoology.

In Linnaeus's time the universal language of science was Latin, and descriptions of animals and plants by zoologists and botanists were routinely published in Latin so that scientists of all nations could understand them. Of course, then, as now, each language had its own vernacular names for many plants and animals, sometimes several local names for the same species. The resulting potential for confusion and misunderstanding is still with us (see, for example, Qs 24 and 30). But even without the confusion, these local names were, and still are, of no use to the international academic community. In pre-Linnaean days the 'official' descriptions of each species usually employed a phrase of several Latin words to define the main features that distinguished it from other species. This phrase would then become the nearest equivalent to an internationally recognised 'name', but since there was no agreed system for devising the phrase, the possibilities for confusion, even among the experts, were enormous.

Linnaeus's simple but brilliant idea was to replace the descriptive phase by a two-part name (hence binomial), still in Latin[2]. The first part, always beginning with a capital letter, is a *genus* name from the Latin word applied to a number of people or things sharing the same origin or several common characteristics. The second part is the *species*[3] name, from the Latin meaning something of a particular kind or appearance and the origin of our English word 'special'[4]. The genus *Homo*[5], to which we humans belong, was considered by Linnaeus, and is still considered, to contain only one living species, ourselves, *Homo sapiens*, meaning 'thinking' or 'wise man'. But other genera (plural of genus) might contain several, perhaps many, broadly similar species with lots of common characteristics. They would all share the same genus name, so that any specialist in that group seeing the name would immediately have a good general idea of what it is like and would then only have to consider the particular features that distinguish it from other members of the same genus. For example, all the big whalebone or rorqual whales are placed in the genus *Balaenoptera*, meaning 'winged whale' and referring to their rather big fins. *Balaenoptera* contains five distinct species ranging from the mighty 30-metre-plus-long (100-foot) blue whale, *Balaenoptera musculus*, whose species name simply means 'muscular', to the much smaller (up to 10-metre-long/33-foot) minke whale, *Balaenoptera acutirostrata*, which means 'sharp-nosed'. The closely related humpback whale is placed in the same family as the other big whales, but is considered sufficiently different from the others to deserve its own separate genus, *Megaptera*, meaning 'big wings' and referring to the humpback's huge fins. Its specific name is *novae-angliae*, meaning 'New England' because when it was first properly described and named in 1781 (though not by Linnaeus) it was thought to be particularly found in New England waters.

Among Linnaeus's many publications (all, of course, in Latin), two are particularly important. These are basically catalogues of all the living creatures known to him, about 5,900 plant species appearing in his *Species Plantarum*, published in 1753,

---

2 Latin being a very beautiful, if dead, language, and Linnaeus being an accomplished Latin scholar, he naturally insisted that the two parts of the name should grammatically agree with one another, the genus being a noun and the species an adjective.

3 In this context the word 'species' applies to both the singular and the plural, a bit like the word *sheep*. So just as you can have one sheep or many sheep, you can also have one species or many species. Nevertheless, you will sometimes hear people who should know better incorrectly using the term *specie* for a single type of animal or plant. But the word 'specie' is actually a more or less obsolete name for coinage or, in the form *in specie*, used in law to mean 'in a very precise or specific sense' – and nothing whatsoever to do with biology.

4 To distinguish it from a genus name, the species name should always start with a lower case letter. Unfortunately, non-technical journalists frequently fail to follow this rule.

5 To emphasise their significance, the Latin names of animals and plants are usually printed in italics.

and 4,400 animal species in the 10th edition of *Systema Naturae* in 1758. Each is considered to be the basis of the naming system used in the two great disciplines of botany and zoology to the present day. At that time, species of animals and plants were more or less universally believed to be separate and unchangeable divine creations. Consequently, the function of Linnaeus's system, like the contemporary less successful naming and classification systems, was considered to be simply to put these entities into some sort of order, much as a librarian might organise books according to their subject matters, authors, or even size or colour. But once Charles Darwin's theory of evolution was generally accepted in the second half of the 19th century, the aim was to discover a 'natural' classification in which the groupings would reflect the degree of relatedness and the evolutionary history of the different species. Closely related species would be grouped into the same genus, related genera would be grouped into the same family, related families into the same super family and so on. Interestingly, but not too surprisingly, the post-Darwinian classifications were often very similar to the earlier ones. After all, Linnaeus's naming and classification system grouped animals and plants together according to their degree of similarity. And since species with a similar evolutionary history, and therefore closely related, will generally share more features in common than less closely related ones, a Linnaean classification would, unintentionally, also tend to be 'natural'. But even if this hadn't been so, Linnaeus's binomial naming system was, and still is, so useful and universally adopted that those unpronounceable Latin names are here to stay and even have sets of rules to help taxonomists produce them sensibly (see Q3)![6]

6   For the real nerds among you, in specialist publications the names of animals or plants may be accompanied by the name or names of the scientist or team of scientists who first described that species and possibly also the date of the original description. For instance, the name of the common dolphin can appear as *Delphinus delphis* Linnaeus, 1758, which tells us that Linnaeus described the common dolphin under this name in 1758 (in *Systema Naturae*). But you may see the author name placed in brackets, as in the scientific name of the blue whale *Balaenoptera musculus* (Linnaeus, 1758). The brackets are placed there not at the whim of the publication's author or editor, but because they have a particular significance, meaning that although Linnaeus described the blue whale (again in *Systema Naturae*, in 1758) and gave it the species name *musculus*, he did not, at that time, place it in the genus *Balaenoptera*. Instead, Linnaeus included the blue whale in his genus *Balaena* along with the Greenland right whale or bowhead, which he called *Balaena mysticetus* and which accordingly still has the name *Balaena mysticetus* Linnaeus, 1758 – with no brackets.
     It wasn't until many years later, in fact in 1864, that the genus name *Balaenoptera* was created to 'house' the rorquals and distinguish them from the right whales, thus resulting in Linnaeus having the brackets put round his name. This important change was made by Dr John Edward Gray, Keeper of Zoology at the Natural History Museum in London from 1840 to 1875, but this fact is not recorded in the blue whale's name, nor are any similar changes recorded in any other animals' official names. In contrast, botanists have a rather more complex nomenclatural system, which provides more information. For example, the scientific name of the channelled wrack, a seaweed forming dense tufts over a wide band on rocky shores in the northern hemisphere, is *Pelvetia canaliculata* (Linnaeus, 1753) Decaisne and Thuret. This tells us that Linnaeus originally described the channelled wrack in his *Species Plantarum* published in 1753, giving it the species name *canaliculata*. However, he placed it in some other genus (his seaweed genus *Fucus*), and it was later transferred to the genus *Pelvetia* by two authors called Decaisne and Thuret.

3 What is the International Code of Zoological Nomenclature?

I must admit that I've never been asked this question in quite this form. But having gone into the formation of zoological names in Q2, and having mentioned the existence of rules, I thought I should put in a bit about them. Since Linnaeus's time, our knowledge of the natural world has increased enormously; for instance, there are now almost 2 million described species of animals compared with Linnaeus's 4,400. Consequently, there has been a huge requirement for new and unique Latin names for all these species, to avoid confusion.

While scientists still routinely used Latin as their *lingua franca* there was no real problem, but during the 19th century Latin lost its pre-eminence as the universal academic language and descriptions of new animals were written in lots of different modern languages, often by zoologists with little or no knowledge of the niceties of Latin[7]. The result was pretty chaotic, with lots of misspellings and zoologists giving several different names to the same species – and sometimes the same name to quite different species. Clearly, some system for regulating the use of names was needed. Fortunately, taxonomists who spend their lives identifying, describing, classifying, cataloguing and naming animals and plants are precisely the nit-picking sorts of people to organise their own regulation. So it won't surprise you to know that since early in the 20th century there has been a set of agreed rules, the *International Code of Zoological Nomenclature*[8], that all zoologists are expected to abide by and, would you believe, a committee, the International Commission on Zoological Nomenclature, to update the code from time to time and to sort out any conflicts.

As you might imagine, the code contains an amazing amount of pedantic stuff about what does and what does not constitute a valid name; how to make the two halves agree; how to use so-called 'barbaric', that is non Latin or Greek, words; how to use proper nouns such as people's names in species names[9]; which name

---

7   Botanists continued to insist on Latin descriptions of new species until well into the 20th century.
8   As you might guess, there is also a code for plant names, the International code of Botanical nomenclature.
9   The names of species and even genera have frequently been made up by 'Latinising' people's names for all sorts of reasons, some laudable, like acknowledging help or inspiration, some less so, like trying to curry favour. I even have two beasts named *ricei* after me, in my case simply because I happened to be the principal scientist on the cruises during which the specimens were originally collected. One of them, *Xylophaga ricei*, is a deep-sea mollusc that makes a living by drilling holes into bits of wood, while the other, *Achaetobonellia ricei*, is also a deep-sea beast, in this case a rather insignificant little worm with a particularly thick integument. So my name will be forever associated with a boring snail and a thick-skinned worm – fame indeed!

takes precedence when one species has been given more than one name – and so on. This probably sounds pretty pathetic and trivial, and some of the arguments taxonomists get into from time to time certainly deserve these epithets. Nevertheless, the objective behind it – to ensure that species are efficiently distinguished between – is always desirable and sometimes crucial. At one extreme it can be a matter of life and death. For instance, there are several examples in which snake bite victims have been treated with antiserum produced from material taken from a misidentified snake, effectively giving the patient a second bite from a different species. At the other extreme, the rules help to dissuade taxonomists from exercising the common human frailty of trying to demonstrate how clever they are, for instance by using excessively long latin word combinations like *anteromedio-basalimagnofasciatipennis*[10].

But the scientific naming of animals is not always as boring as you might think, and despite the rules there are lots of amusing stories associated with it. Here's one of my favourites.

My period at the Natural History Museum in London corresponded with the acquisition of the institution's first scanning electron microscope (SEM), an instrument devised to look at the structure of small objects by firing electrons at them rather than the light beams used in conventional optical microscopes for the previous three hundred years. The results were revolutionary, providing images of tiny creatures with an almost limitless depth of focus and allowing scientists to see features that had previously been totally invisible. Some of my museum pals studying the arachnids – that is, the group that includes ticks, mites and spiders – embraced the new technology enthusiastically, sometimes with dramatic results. One of the early targets was a previously undescribed species of a soil mite belonging to the well-known genus *Steganacarus*. When they looked at the SEM images they were amazed to see that the creature's upper surface, what you might call its back, instead of being pretty flat and featureless, as it appeared through a light microscope, in fact had a huge circular depression or hole in it, a structure never seen before and clearly worth making a bit of a fuss about. At the time, there was a very high-profile television advertising campaign for the popular peppermint sweet, Polo mints, using the very successful and widely known catchphrase 'Polo, the mint with a hole'. My arachnid mates thought this was too good a coincidence to miss, so when they had prepared their detailed description of the new species for publication, they submitted it to the appropriate academic journal under the

10 Meaning something like 'having large bundles of feathers on the under side of the middle parts of the front regions! I don't know whether anyone has ever tried to use such a daft word as a species name, but if they did, the Commission would understandably take a very dim view of it.

title 'Steganacarus polo, the mite with a hole'. To his eternal shame, the journal editor had a poorly developed sense of humour and insisted that the name be changed, so Steganacarus polo sadly does not exist!

4 What are red tides?

Quite a few of the questions in Do Whales...? were about marine plants. They dealt particularly with the tiny plant cells forming the phytoplankton, the drifting communities found throughout the surface layers of the oceans and performing the crucial role of capturing the energy in sunlight to produce complex molecules in the process of photosynthesis. In doing so they provide the basic food on which almost all the oceans' animal communities depend. But sometimes you can have too much of a good thing, and red tides are one of the results.

Red tide is a general term for a phenomenon in which the tiny phytoplankton cells become locally so numerous that they cause discoloration of the water. The discoloration is caused by the concentration of pigments in the algal cells and, although these are often red, sometimes extremely so, they can also range through orange and yellow to brown and green, depending on which species are involved. Since these blooms can occur in fresh water as well as in the sea, and in the open ocean as well as in estuarine and inshore waters, the use of the word 'tide' is also not very appropriate.

The algal blooms can often be harmful and the term 'harmful algal bloom' is used increasingly instead of the more traditional 'red tide'. The harmful effects are usually the result of the production of natural toxins by the algae, which can have serious consequences on wildlife and on man, particularly because the toxins can accumulate in commercially exploited molluscan shellfish such as oysters and mussels. However, in addition to these toxic effects, some algal blooms can be so concentrated that they clog the gills of fish and shellfish and their decaying remains can deplete the oxygen concentration in the water to lethal levels.

Although these algal blooms can occur almost anywhere and at any time, they are a particularly regular feature of some localities. One of the best studied is the so-called Florida red tide, an almost annual phenomenon of the Gulf of Mexico region. It is caused by a tiny planktonic plant named Karenia brevis, which can achieve densities of tens of millions of cells per litre of seawater. Karenia brevis produces a neurotoxin called brevitoxin, which can be concentrated in shellfish and have serious consequences for people who eat affected animals such as clams and mussels. The toxins can also be carried in the wind as an aerosol, causing chronic respiratory problems.

Algal blooms came to global attention in June 2008, just before the Olympic Games, when the sea off Qingdao, where the Olympic sailing events were to be held, was subjected to a huge increase in algal biomass, though in this case distinctly green. Local scientists attributed the bloom to increased rainfall and warmer waters in the Yellow Sea.

Whether this was true or not, the cause of algal blooms is often uncertain, though a sudden and local increase in the availability of nutrients is usually involved. Like their terrestrial equivalents, marine plants, including phytoplanktonic algae, are dependent for growth upon sufficient sunlight, adequate warmth and the availability of nutrients such as phosphates and nitrates. In most circumstances, particularly in seasonal temperate seas, the increasing sunlight in the spring allows the overwintering algal cells to grow fairly rapidly and produce a spring algal bloom. But the herbivorous zooplanktonic animals graze the algae and prevent the bloom from reaching 'red tide' concentrations, in much the same way that grazing sheep and cows prevent a meadow from becoming totally overgrown. In a red tide situation, the injection of nutrients is either too rapid or at the wrong time to allow the grazers to control the growth.

The source of the nutrients can be a result of human activity. For example, algal blooms in freshwater lakes are often caused by run-off from agricultural lands carrying fertiliser into the water body. In the same way, rivers flowing through agricultural landscapes can carry high levels of nutrients to the sea and stimulate algal blooms as a consequence. On the other hand, some blooms seem to be entirely natural and caused by local wind and current conditions causing upwelling of sub-surface water and injecting high levels of natural nutrients into the upper water column.

Although red tides are normally restricted to shallow continental shelf waters, they can occur in the open sea where they may form long narrow patches of discoloration, which have probably been 'fed' by upwelling between two adjacent water currents. But these should not be confused with the concentrations of floating material resulting from Langmuir circulation, which is a quite distinct phenomenon (see Q76).

5 What are foraminiferans and radiolarians?

The foraminiferans (or forams for short) and the radiolarians are two groups of tiny and relatively simple organisms, which older readers might have come across as vague relatives of *Amoeba*, a representative of the now defunct group the

Protozoa meaning 'first animals'. Because they are so small, you will almost certainly never see a living member of either group. So why should you bother to find out anything about them? Well, apart from the fact that they are particularly beautiful creatures (see Fig 1), for at least three fairly closely related reasons: first, because they play a crucial role in the way the oceans work; second, because they may be particularly important in determining how the earth responds to global warming; and third, their skeletal remains form the bulk of deep-sea sediments and carry a record of the earth's climatic past (see Q42).

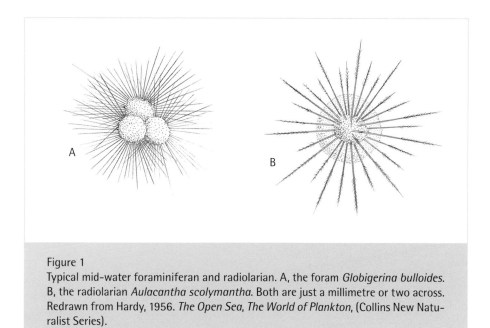

Figure 1
Typical mid-water foraminiferan and radiolarian. A, the foram *Globigerina bulloides*. B, the radiolarian *Aulacantha scolymantha*. Both are just a millimetre or two across. Redrawn from Hardy, 1956. *The Open Sea, The World of Plankton*, (Collins New Naturalist Series).

The old classification of almost all living beings into two major divisions, or kingdoms – that is, either plants or animals – is no longer used because many groups seem to blur the boundaries between them. Nevertheless, the foraminiferans and radiolarians are definitely well into the old animal division since they do not produce complex molecules themselves, like true plants, but need to eat organic material ranging from bacteria to the living or dead remains of other organisms.

Both groups live throughout the water column and, in the case of forams, also on the sea floor. A bit like an *Amoeba*, forams and radiolarians extrude tiny cytoplasmic filaments both to feed and to move. Unlike *Amoeba*, however, both forams and radiolarians have rigid skeletons to support and protect the protoplasm. In the foraminiferans the skeleton takes the form of a shell consisting of one or more chambers, a bit like a snail. And also like snails, foram shells are usually made up mainly of calcium carbonate, though many of the ones living on the sea floor also accumulate bits of sediment into their shells. The name foraminiferan refers to the fact that the shell is usually pierced by lots of foramens or holes through which the animal's protoplasm protrudes.

In contrast to the forams, the skeletons of most radiolarians are made up of silica or glass, though one group has a skeleton of strontium sulphate. The name radiolarian refers to the fact that the skeletons of many of them have a central, more or less spherical capsule with needle-like spicules radiating in all directions and supporting a frothy mass of cytoplasm. There are several hundreds of radiolarian species in the oceans with skeletons in a bewildering variety of exquisite shapes, many of them looking rather like snowflakes.

Both foraminiferans and radiolarians can occur in vast numbers and, after death, their skeletons sink to the bottom of the sea, where their remains often dominate the sediments. The best-known foraminiferans belong to the genus *Globigerina*, whose multi-chambered globular chalky skeletons form the bulk of the sediments over large areas of the deep sea floor, where they form so-called 'Globigerina oozes'. In the deeper parts of the oceans, particularly at depths in excess of about 4,000m (13,000ft), the high pressure causes the chalky calcareous shells – such as those of the foraminiferans – to dissolve, leaving behind sediments dominated by the glassy remains of radiolarians. The resulting radiolarian oozes are particularly abundant at high latitudes in the Pacific Ocean and in the equatorial regions of both the Pacific and Indian Oceans.

Deep-sea sediments accumulate very slowly, mostly at just a few centimetres per 1,000 years. So where the sediment is hundreds of metres thick, as it is in many regions of the ocean, it represents many millions of years of sedimentation[11]. Long cores of these sediments collected by ocean scientists provide a sort of tape recording of the history of the oceans over very long time periods. This is partly because different species of forams and radiolarians, many of which have changed very little over millions of years, are known to favour particular oceanic conditions. Accordingly, as the relative abundances of the remains of different species change in the cores, they indicate associated changes in the overlying water column. But even more importantly, the skeletal remains – especially of the forams – amazingly retain a record of the water temperature at the time when they were alive and are therefore extremely useful in indicating past climatic changes. And the key to this record is oxygen. This is a bit complicated but worth persevering with, as it is so important in understanding how climate scientists can claim to know what happened many thousands of years ago.

---

11   The oldest oceanic sediments so far recovered from the oceans are from the late Jurassic Period, some 150–160 million years ago.

Oxygen has three stable isotopes – that is, three forms of the oxygen atom, each with different numbers of neutrons. The significance of this from our point of view is simply that the three isotopes have slightly different weights. The lightest form, ^{16}O, is by far the most abundant, making up well over 99% of naturally occurring oxygen. The next heaviest, ^{17}O, is pretty rare in nature and for our purposes can be ignored. But the heaviest form, ^{18}O, though also pretty rare at about 0.2% of the total naturally occuring oxygen, varies in abundance according to changes in temperature.

Oxygen makes up 90% of water by weight, but because the most abundant isotope, ^{16}O, is lighter, when water evaporates it is lost more easily than ^{18}O. The result is that the water vapour in the atmosphere is dominated even more by ^{16}O, while leaving behind water with a tiny bit more of the heavier stuff. So the more evaporation is taking place, usually a reflection of temperature, the higher the proportion of heavy ^{18}O in the water. When animals like the mid-water forams make their chalky shells of calcium carbonate, that is $CaCO_3$, the O_3 bit is made up of oxygen with the isotope ratio characteristic of the water temperature surrounding them. When they die, and their shells sink to the bottom, this ratio is locked up for all time – or until an oceanographer comes along and uses a clever bit of chemistry to unlock it. But – and this is probably even more important than allowing scientists to determine how the temperatures of the upper ocean layers have altered in the past – the oxygen isotope in the remains of some beasts can indicate how much water was locked up in glaciers at the time, giving an idea of global climatic changes.

This is because, even when the global temperature is low, the water vapour in the atmosphere is enriched in ^{16}O and depleted in ^{18}O because of the evaporation effect, while the reverse will be true of the seawater left behind. During glacial periods this water vapour is precipitated as snow and builds up to form the glaciers and ice caps, all with oxygen isotope ratios that are characteristic of the atmosphere at the time. And the bigger the ice caps – that is, the more intense the global cooling – the bigger will be the difference between the isotope ratio in the ice compared with that in the sea.

Now we have to go back to the foram remains preserved in the sediments. As we saw above, the isotope ratios in the shells of upper ocean mid-water forams reflect the changing temperature in the water column. But the ones living on the bottom of the deep ocean, where the water temperature is pretty constant and cold no matter what is happening high above them, have oxygen isotope ratios that tend to reflect the global seawater ratio, unaffected by the vagaries of minor temperature changes. Consequently, these bottom-living or 'benthic' foram shells provide a superb record of the past changes in the amount of water held in the world's ice sheets[12].

12   For more detailed information, see Summerhayes and Thorpe, 1996, *Oceanography: An Illustrated Guide*, Manson Publishing.

6 Are corals animals?

Yes, they are. But it took scientists a long time to realise this – not much more than a couple of hundred years ago most people thought corals were strange underwater plants.

Corals belong to a major animal group (phylum) called the Cnidaria by zoologists[13]. The name comes from the Greek word *knide*, meaning 'nettle', and refers to the fact that almost all cnidarians possess curious stinging structures called cnidocytes, which they use to capture and subdue their food or for defence against potential predators.

The Cnidaria contains about 9,000 known species, all aquatic and the vast majority found only in the oceans. They contain some of the most beautiful of all marine creatures, but also some of the most deadly (see Q7). Although they can assume the most amazing shapes and colours, the basic body plan of all cnidarians is extremely simple. They consist of two 'skin' layers, one inner, one outer, and each usually only one cell thick, with the bulk of the animal made up of a jelly-like substance, called mesoglea, between the two layers. Most more advanced animals, including us, have a third, intermediate layer of cells called the mesoderm, from which most of our complex organs are derived. But based on the more simple system, cnidarians come in two apparently quite different body forms, a mobile type that swim freely in the water, and a stationary type that live attached to something else such as the sea floor or another animal or plant. The mobile forms include all those creatures known broadly as jellyfish (see Fig 2), while the stationary ones include the sea anemones, sea pens and corals. Both forms are radially symmetrical; that is, instead of having an obvious front or head end and rear end like most animals, they are built on a circular plan so that they could theoretically be cut into a series of very similar slices, a bit like a pizza[14].

The basic unit of all of these groups is called a polyp, from the Latin word *polypus* meaning 'many-footed', though in the cnidarians it refers to the fact that they have many tentacles rather than feet. The sea anemones found in intertidal rock pools are excellent examples of polyps. Each anemone consists of a simple cup-like body with the 'rim' of the cup fringed by a number, sometimes hundreds, of tentacles, each armed with lots of stinging cells. When the tide is out, sea anemones look pretty unprepossessing, being reduced to a blob of rather unattractive jelly. But when they are submerged in water the body expands and

---

13   Readers of a certain age may be more familiar with the name Coelenterata, which is now defunct.
14   This body plan is not unique to the Cnidaria, of course. It is also found in another very successful marine group, the echinoderms, which includes sea urchins, starfish and brittlestars (see Q8).

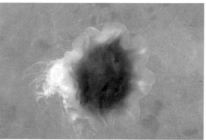

Figure 2
Two common jellyfish, the moon jelly (*Aurelia aurita*, left) and the lion's mane jelly (*Cyanea capillata*, right). Both species are widespread in the North Atlantic and Mediterranean and have close relatives in the other oceans. The moon jelly, reaching about 30cm (12in) across, is harmless to humans. In contrast, the lion's mane reaches a metre (3ft) or more across with stinging tentacles up to 15m (50ft) long. Its sting is extremely powerful and, while not deadly, can be very painful and could have serious consequences for anyone with a heart condition.

Figure 3
Beadlet anemones, *Actinia equina*, photographed in a rock pool on the shore at Freshwater on the coast of Pembrokeshire, South Wales (expanded left, contracted right). Beadlets grow to about 5cm (2 in) across and are usually red, though they can be green, brown or orange.

the tentacles fan out so that they look like the petals of a brightly coloured flower, hence the common name (see Fig 3).

The space inside the cup, or body cavity, is filled with seawater and has only one opening to the outside, a 'mouth' in the middle of the ring of tentacles. Food particles captured by the tentacles are passed through the mouth into the body cavity, where they are broken down by digestive enzymes secreted by cells of the lining layer and then absorbed by the same layer, a bit like our own gut lining. But in the absence of an anus, all indigestible waste material has to be thrown out through the mouth. At the same time, the stale seawater is exchanged for fresh, oxygen-filled water because the body cavity also does the job of respiration, with the lining cells absorbing oxygen and giving off carbon dioxide, just like our lungs. Finally, the lining of the body cavity also carries the reproductive organs, the gonads. The eggs and sperm are shed through the mouth into the sea. The fertilised eggs will develop into tiny cigar-shaped larvae that swim around using tiny hairs called cilia. Eventually, with a lot of luck, they will find a suitable place to settle and will become attached by one end and develop into a new sea anemone to begin the cycle all over again.

Much the same happens with corals but, unlike sea anemones, corals are mostly – but not exclusively – colonial. This means that hundreds or thousands of polyps are joined together into a single living unit. The ones that build the familiar tropical coral reefs secrete a hard external skeleton made of calcium carbonate, with lots of separate little depressions each holding an individual polyp. As the colony grows, the underlying stony mass gets bigger and bigger, the shape and detailed structure depending on the individual species. But in all cases the living tissue is restricted to a very thin surface veneer, with the bulk of the underlying material being the non-living skeletal remains of former generations of polyps, sometimes going back thousands of years.

Although coral polyps catch food particles with their tentacles just like sea anemones, the tropical reef-building ones get at least some of their food from tiny specialised photosynthetic algal cells called zooxanthellae, living inside the coral. This mutually advantageous relationship, or symbiosis, provides the alga with a secure place to live and the coral with a home-grown food supply. But it also means that the reef builders can live only where the sunlight is bright enough for their algal partners to grow, which explains why living reefs are found only in relatively shallow water.

Despite all this, don't run away with the idea that reef-building corals are restricted to shallow tropical waters. They are not, and some of the world's biggest reefs are on the deep sea floor at depths of 1,000m (3,280ft) or more and in water temperatures not much above zero. These reefs have been known about since the 1860s, but their true extent and significance has become apparent only in the last 30 or 40 years. They are probably to be found all over the world, but they are best known from the north-eastern Atlantic where, like tropical reefs, some of them are thought to be thousands of years old. With the expansion of fishing into deeper and deeper waters, these venerable reefs are extremely susceptible to trawl damage. Fortunately, help seems to be at hand, not least because

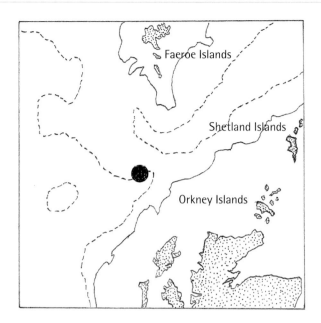

Figure 4
A strange place for a coral reef! The area of the Darwin Mounds (the black dot) in the deep water between the Faeroes and Scotland. The solid line is the 200-metre (655-foot) contour (or isobath) and the dotted line is the 1,000-metre (3,280-foot) contour.

the word 'reef' seems to carry a lot of weight with both the public and politicians. As a result, one of the largest known areas of deep cold-water reefs, the Darwin Mounds, in the deep Atlantic some 180km (112 miles) to the north-west of Scotland's Cape Wrath (see Fig 4), have now received official protection from the European Union. The mounds or bumps in the sea floor, typically about 5m (16ft) high and 100 or so metres (328ft) in diameter, cover an area of more than 100 square kilometres (40 square miles) at a depth of about 1,000m (3,280ft) and harbour a range of fascinating creatures, including cold-water corals. They were discovered in the 1990s by oceanographers on board the British Research vessel RRS *Charles Darwin* – hence the name – and have been studied fairly intensively since that time using underwater cameras and sidescan sonar (see Q73). Unfortunately, these studies revealed that a good deal of the area had already been severely damaged by heavy deep-sea trawls, and coral material thought to be as old as 4,500 years was obtained from commercial trawl catches in the area.

Following representations by scientists and environmental pressure groups, the mounds were given permanent protection by EU Fisheries Ministers in 2004 and trawling in the area is now banned.

7 Do sea wasps sting?

They certainly do, and the effects are generally much worse that those of their terrestrial namesakes.

Sea wasps are jellyfish belonging to a small group called the Cubozoa or 'box jellies' because their bodies have four flat sides, a bit like a cube or box. The Cubozoa contains about 15 species, all found in tropical or subtropical waters and mainly in Australasia and south-east Asia. Although all of the species are toxic, one – *Chironex fleckeri,* the true sea wasp – is particularly poisonous and may deserve the title as the most venomous creature on earth.

The sea wasp's transparent box-shaped body can be up to 25cm (10in) across and weigh up to 2kg (4.4lbs). Each lower 'corner' of the box carries a cluster of 16 tentacles up to 3m (10ft) long, each carrying thousands of stinging cells. Sea wasps occur in inshore waters and river mouths of the eastern coasts of Australia and Malaysia, particularly during the southern summer, from November to March. The poison causes complete circulatory failure and respiratory paralysis. If untreated, death can occur within minutes.

A much smaller, but almost equally dangerous box jelly is the thumbnail-sized Irukandji jellyfish, *Carukia barnesi,* named for the Irukandji people whose traditional territory stretches along the coastal strip north of Cairns in Queensland, where the jellies seem to be particularly prevalent.

The effects of the stings of these jellies, particularly from the Irukandji jelly, are called, would you believe, the Irukandji syndrome. Typically, the symptoms include excruciating pain, especially muscle cramps in the limbs, along with sweating, nausea, severe headaches and vomiting, as well as very disturbing psychological trauma. The sting itself is rarely particularly debilitating, but the resulting symptoms, developing from about half an hour after the initial attack, may last for several days and require hospitalisation. Although the use of antihistamines to control inflammation and a variety of painkilling drugs is usually effective, unless treatment is started relatively quickly the effects can be very serious indeed, and several deaths have been recorded. If I were you, I would stay safely out of the water at these times!

8 What are the echinoderms?

The word 'echinoderm' is derived from two Greek words meaning 'spiny skin', and is applied to a huge group of animals without backbones, including starfish, brittlestars and sea urchins, all restricted to the oceans and not found at all in freshwater.

In addition to these relatively familiar groups, the echinoderms also includes two rather less widely known groups, the sea cucumbers and the sea lilies, also called feather stars. Sea cucumbers, as the name suggests, are generally elongated and a bit cucumber-like in appearance, growing up to 50cm long, though usually much smaller. Sea lilies, in contrast, have a superficial resemblance to a flower, hence their name, because they are rather like a many armed, stalked brittlestar more or less firmly attached to rocks or seabed sediment.

Most echinoderms are radially symmetrical, that is with their bodies built on a circular plan a bit like a pizza. But whereas you could cut the average pizza into any number of slices, all of them more or less identical, echinoderms are usually pentamerous so that most of the body parts are repeated five times around the 'circle'. This is why most starfish and brittlestars have five arms, though in some species they are subdivided into twenty or more. In some groups the radial symmetry is modified to produce a superficial bilateral symmetry, that is with a front and back end and right and left sides just like more 'normal' animals. This is obvious in the sea cucumbers with their elongated shape, and rather less so in the heart urchins, a group of mainly sand and mud dwelling sea urchins in which the usual circular form becomes somewhat heart shaped with a definite front and back end. Nevertheless, in both cases the detailed anatomy shows that, like all their echinoderm relatives, they are built on a pentamerous radial symmetry.

Because all echinoderms have chalky skeletal plates, and frequently lots of hard spines, they have left an excellent fossil record. From these fossils it is clear that the group has been around for a very long time, the earliest members appearing more than 500 million years ago. Although they have never conquered fresh water nor, of course, the land, they are an extremely successful marine group, occurring from the intertidal zone to the bottoms of the deepest ocean trenches. In fact, the sea cucumbers are often the most abundant and easily recognisable creatures in films or photographs of the deep sea floor.

While the vast majority of the 7,000 or so modern echinoderm species live on or in the seabed sediments or crawl over rocks or other seafloor animals and plants, a few species of brittlestars and sea lilies can swim quite effectively, at least for short periods. And a few sea cucumber species, particularly in the deep ocean, have adopted the swimming mid-water lifestyle completely.

Echinoderms have adopted more or less all possible feeding styles. These include herbivores, living and feeding on large seaweeds or grazing tiny algae from rock surfaces; predators actively seeking out living prey animals such as bivalve molluscs; carrion feeders specialising on eating dead carcasses; detritivores specialised for feeding on tiny particles sinking to the sea floor; and finally suspension feeders depending upon small floating food particles that they filter out of the water as it drifts past them.

Because there is not a great deal to the average echinoderm apart from chalky plates and a lot of spines, humans have never exploited them for food in the way they have most other animal groups. Nevertheless, some choice parts of echinoderms, particularly the gonads or roes of sea urchins and sea cucumbers, are considered delicacies in Mediterranean countries and in Asia. However, whenever I have had the opportunity to sample them I have always found them to be vastly over-rated – not to say appalling. But don't let me put you off!

9 What makes a crab a crab?

Answering this question can't be at the top of many people's wish list. After all, few of us will have given much thought to crabs in general except as a potential filling for sandwiches. Until, that is, Discovery Channel's *Deadliest Catch* television series burst onto the small screen in 2005. Now in its sixth season and transmitted in more than 150 countries worldwide, the programmes document the extremely dangerous – but highly entertaining – events surrounding the Alaskan crab fishery, mainly around the Aleutian Islands and based on the port of Dutch Harbor, Alaska. Suddenly, crabs became flavour of the month, so to speak, and quite a few people started to ask me what exactly *are* the huge creatures being pulled up in enormous traps by the *Deadliest Catch* fishermen. Unfortunately, like many seemingly simple questions, this one doesn't have a simple answer. So before looking at this specific problem, let's look first at what makes a crab a crab.

This may sound a pretty daft question. Surely everybody knows a crab when they see one? Well, yes, but that's not the same as knowing what makes a crab a crab, partly because most of us are familiar with very few different sorts of crabs, mainly the ones on a fishmonger's stall on the one hand and the little devils that kids catch at the seaside on the other (Fig 5). So let's look at a few more crabs – both real ones and imposters!

All crabs are arthropods – that is, they have a hard outer shell and jointed legs (which is what 'arthropod' means), and share lots of features with other arthropods like the insects and arachnids (ticks, mites and spiders). But whereas the insects

Figure 5
The velvet swimming crab, *Necora puber*, in its normal surroundings among intertidal rocks and seaweed (left), and aggressively grabbing a walking stick and
showing its flattened paddle-like last pair of legs (right). Like its close rocky-shore
relative the green or common shore crab, it grows to about 8cm (3 in) across. But
whereas the shore crab is usually rather shy and retiring, the velvet swimming
crab is very pugnacious and, if disturbed, will stand very upright with its claws
outstretched and ready for action.

and arachnids are primarily terrestrial creatures, the crabs and their close relatives
are separated off in a third great arthropod division, the crustaceans, which are
mostly aquatic[15]. Compared with the 1 million or so described species of insects,
the 50-odd thousand known crustacean species are pretty insignificant. Nevertheless, the crustaceans include a vast range of animals, many of which are crucial
constituents of freshwater and marine communities and help to make them tick.
Even the most ardent crab lover would not claim this sort of importance for them,
but quite a few crab species and their ten-legged crustacean relatives are highly
regarded as human food around the world. These ten-legged beasts, or decapods,
include the shrimps, prawns and lobsters, all dealt with in *Do Whales...?* and all
with long tails, the bits that we eat. But the decapods also contain a number of
groups with short or seemingly non-existent tails, including the true crabs and
some slightly 'less than true' crabs.

The real or true crabs all belong to a group called the *Brachyura*, a name made
up from two Greek words, *brachys* meaning 'short' and *oura* meaning 'tail'. They
all fold their five-segmented tails tightly beneath the body, between the bases of
the legs, so that viewed from above the tail is completely invisible. But if you turn
the crab upside down you can see the tail clearly as a series of shelly plates, usually
broad in females (for carrying the eggs) and narrow in males. In both sexes,

15   But crustaceans are by no means exclusively aquatic, and some of our most familiar terrestrial arthro-
     pods, the woodlice or pill bugs, are crustaceans.

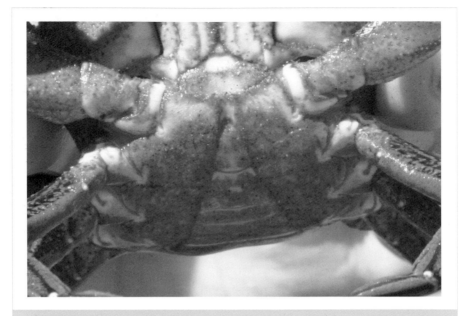

Figure 6
The underside of a male velvet swimming crab showing the triangular tail folded
forwards between the bases of the legs. In a female the tail would be much broader,
with rounded sides.

however, the grooves marking the divisions between the tail segments run regularly from side to side like the rungs of a ladder (see Fig 6).

Worldwide, there are approaching 5,000 described species of true crab. Most of them live in the sea, from the shoreline to depths of 2,000m (6,560ft) or more, where some of the most remarkable crab species form part of the amazing communities around hydrothermal vents. But some crabs live in fresh water and a few spend much of their adult lives on dry land[16].

Adult true crabs range in size from tiny beasts only a few millimetres across and living inside other creatures such as mussels and corals, to monsters weighing

16   Probably the most publicized land crabs are those on Christmas Island in the Indian Ocean. Here, two
      species in particular – the red land crab *Gecarcoidea natalis* (the species name referring to Christmas)
      and the blue land crab *Cardisoma hirtipes* – occur in such huge numbers that, at times, they dominate
      the island's ecology, even affecting the human population. For instance, the Christmas Island golf club
      is the only one in the world to have specific rules to deal with obstructions caused by crabs! For more
      details, see *Christmas Crabs* by John Hicks, Holger Rumpff and Hugh Yorkston, published in 1984 by
      the Christmas Island Natural History Association.

many kilos. The biggest of all are the Tasmanian giant crab, *Pseudocarcinus gigas*, which, as its common name suggests, lives in southern Australasian waters, and the giant Japanese spider crab, *Macrocheira kaempferi*, which, equally obviously, lives around Japan. The Tasmanian giant crab reaches a carapace (that is, shell) width of about 45cm (18in) and can weigh as much as 13kg (29lb). But even this goliath pales into relative insignificance in comparison with its Japanese cousin. Although the shell of a big Japanese spider crab is no bigger than that of the Tasmanian one, it sits in the centre of an array of enormously long legs, hence the spider epithet. In fact, with a maximum leg span of almost 4m (13ft) from claw to claw, the Japanese spider crab has the greatest leg span of any arthropod and is much bigger than any spider[17]. Despite its fearsome appearance, it seems to be a bit of a pussycat in its natural environment, feeding on relatively small shellfish (that is, molluscs and crustaceans), living on the sea floor and scavenging carcasses. Nevertheless, it is fished commercially and I can imagine that a thump from one of its flailing claws in the bottom of a small fishing boat could be quite painful. However, catching a 3- or 4-metre (10- or 13-foot) giant seems to be a pretty rare event these days, and the average size of crabs caught by fishermen have leg spans of not much more than a metre (3ft) or so[18].

Lots of species of true crab are exploited commercially and eaten around the world, but in the northern hemisphere two species dominate the catches. These are the edible crab in the North Atlantic and Mediterranean and the Dungeness crab in the North Pacific (Fig 7). The European edible crab was given the Latin name *Cancer pagurus* by Carl Linnaeus (see Q2) in the 18th century, whereas the Dungeness crab was not described until 1852. It was given the scientific name *Cancer magister*, simply meaning 'master crab', though it has now been moved to a different genus, *Metacarcinus*. It gets its common name from the town of Dungeness[19] in the state of Washington, where the first processing plants were established. The crab is harvested along the whole of the west coast of the United States and plays such an important role in the economy of the state of Oregon that, in 2009, it was designated as the state crustacean. Clearly some crabs have friends in high places!

Finally, we can try to answer the *Deadliest Catch* crab question, because the fishery is for two quite distinct groups of 'crab' species, all of them pretty large

---

17   Thank goodness! After all, a true spider this size would be an awesome sight. The Japanese spider crab can reach its enormous size only because, in life, its body is supported by the water in which it lives. In air it would be quite incapable of moving effectively.

18   Nevertheless, in February 2010 a Japanese spider crab with a 3-metre (10-foot) leg span, and almost inevitably dubbed 'crabzilla' by the press, was reported as being housed temporarily at Birmingham's National Sea Life Centre in the UK before being transferred to its permanent home in Belgium.

19   Washington's Dungeness presumably got its name from the Dungeness in Kent of which, apparently, the New York Times endearingly said, 'If Kent is the garden of England, Dungeness is the back gate.'

Figure 7
Dungeness crabs, *Metacarcinus magister*, offered live and on ice at the world-famous Pike Street market in Seattle.

and mostly taken for their long, meat-filled legs. One of these groups – the snow crabs, belonging to the spider crab genus *Chionoecetes* – are true crabs and are more or less closely related to the giant Japanese spider crab. But the other group, which form by far the most important part of the Alaskan fishery catches, are not proper crabs at all. Instead, they belong to the family Lithodidae or stone crabs, which are more closely related to the snail-shell-occupying hermit crabs than to the true crabs. Three species are targeted, the highly prized red king crab, *Paralithodes camtschaticus*[20] and the rather less sought-after blue king crab *Paralithodes platypus* and golden king crab *Lithodes aequispinus*.

I doubt if anyone would ever challenge the right to market these species as 'crab' without the 'hermit' qualifier, and in any case I imagine few people could tell the difference in taste. Nevertheless, if you wanted confirmation that they are descended from hermit crabs you would need to look fairly closely at their fifth

20   Red king crabs are naturally restricted to the North Pacific. However, in the 1960s they were introduced into the Barents Sea by Russian fisheries scientists hoping to improve the local maritime resources. The crabs not only survived, but had a huge population explosion and have spread into Norwegian waters where they are widely considered an unwanted pest.

pair of legs and at the hard shelly covering of the tail, which is tucked between the bases of the legs, just like true crabs. This is very different from the tails of most hermit crabs, where the tail is soft and very vulnerable and is coiled around inside an empty marine snail shell for protection. Millions of years ago the hermit crab ancestors had fairly normal, and straight, lobster-like tails. So in order to get their tails into the coiled shell, modern hermits have evolved twisted and asymmetrical tails. And they have also had to adapt their walking legs so that the fifth pair, at least, is always much smaller than the rest. Evolution of the stone crabs seems to have abandoned the tail-in-shell approach to security in favour of the more traditional 'crab' solution of tucking the tail under the tummy – but the telltale signs of a hermit ancestry are still there. First, like true hermits, the stone crabs have insignificant fifth legs, certainly no good for eating. But the best evidence is in the tail, where the joints in the shell between the original segments are not at all like the rungs of a ladder but are skewed at funny angles, revealing their asymmetrical and twisted past!

I could carry on and bore you with accounts of lots of other less-than-true crabs, like frog crabs and mole crabs, but nobody has made a TV series about them, so I won't. Nevertheless, what I have included has hopefully convinced you that 'What is a crab?' is not quite as daft a question as it seemed.

10 What are barnacles?

Anyone who has ever walked over a rocky shore will be only too aware of barnacles, not least because if you fall over on the shore it is the sharp shells of the barnacles that are likely to scrape off your skin as effectively as a file. In most places the 'file' would be fairly fine because most intertidal barnacles are no more than a centimetre (less than half an inch) across and a similar height. But in some areas, for example the North Pacific, the shore barnacles can be well over 3cm (an inch or so) high (see Fig 8), while deeper still they can reach a length of 10cm (4in) or more.

Barnacles come in two basic forms: acorn barnacles, the ones we've just been discussing, which are stuck directly on to rocks, pilings or ships' bottoms and look a bit like tiny limpets; and goose barnacles, attached via a long stalk which is edible and considered something of a delicacy in many Mediterranean countries. Goose barnacles are often found on floating bits and pieces including lumps of wood, buoys and so on. But they can also live attached to rocks, just like their acorn barnacle relatives (see Fig 9).

Despite the limpet-like appearance of acorn barnacles, they are emphatically *not* molluscs. Nor are the goose barnacles. All of them are crustaceans and are

Figure 8
This pair of huge acorn barnacles, each about 4cm (1½in) across, was photo-graphed on the shore at Icy Point, Alaska. They are not snuggling up to one another by chance! See text.

related to the crabs, shrimps and lobsters, though the resemblance is not very obvious. The giveaway is their legs, normally completely hidden inside the shell – along with all the rest of the intertidal acorn barnacle's soft bits – when the tide is out. But if you see them underwater you get a completely different impression. Every couple of seconds a little hand-like object pops in and out of the hole at the apex of the shell. Under a microscope you would see that the 'hand' is made up of a series of hairy little jointed bristles. These are the barnacle's legs and they are built on exactly the same plan as shrimp or crab legs. However, in the barnacle's case they are used not for walking or swimming, but for feeding, because the barnacle uses its legs to filter tiny food particles drifting past it in the water, effectively kicking them into its mouth. Goose barnacles are a bit different because they spread their hairy legs outside their shells like a net to catch food particles as the water flows through it. They periodically withdraw the net and lick off any collected food.

All this was unknown until a couple of hundred years ago. Before that, not only did naturalists not realise that barnacles are crustaceans, but goose barnacles in particular were the subject of some very strange ideas. In the medieval world

Figure 9
Goose barnacles (on the right and upper left) and acorn barnacles (lower left) photographed on the shore of Victoria Island, British Columbia.

there was a somewhat fanciful perceived resemblance between goose barnacles and proper geese. The two groups were believed to be related, hence the names 'goose barnacle' and 'barnacle goose'. And when the geese mysteriously and suddenly disappeared, then equally suddenly reappeared at the beginning and end of what we now know is their annual migration, the medieval savants decided that during their absence they were adopting a marine existence in the form of the barnacles. Unlikely as this seemed, it was rather convenient. After all, if geese turned into barnacles they must surely be fish and not birds. So they were excluded from the religious ban on eating meat on Fridays and made a welcome addition to the permissible food – but only, of course, for those fortunates who could afford them.

Charles Darwin was fascinated by barnacles and studied them for many years. Like most barnacle specialists he was impressed by their reproductive anatomy. The vast majority of barnacles are hermaphrodite – that is, each individual contains both male and female sex organs. But as for all animals and plants, self-fertilisation is not a good idea because it leads to a reduction in the gene pool. The solution for acorn barnacles is to have, size for size, probably the longest penises in the animal kingdom, enabling them to fertilise their neighbours despite being immovably stuck down! No wonder they snuggle up, so to speak. You would never guess at the goings on between those little beasts as you walk across the rocks, would you?

11 What is the blue-ringed octopus?

Octopuses are molluscs, and are placed in the same major division, the cephalopods (meaning 'head-footed'), that also contains squid and cuttlefish. There are about 300 known species of octopuses, ranging from tiny creatures a few centimetres across to huge beasts with arm spans of several metres. The biggest species is almost certainly the North Pacific giant octopus, *Enteroctopus dofleini*, which certainly reaches an arm span of 4–5m (13–16ft) and possibly considerably more. All octopuses are marine, being found from the intertidal zone to the deep ocean and feeding on a wide range of food, mostly invertebrates like themselves but sometimes taking fish. They all have quite powerful jaws or beaks at the centre of the arms and most, if not all, can inflict a venomous bite. Nevertheless, most octopuses are very timid and represent no significant threat to man. Quite the reverse, in fact, since octopus features significantly in the cuisine of many parts of the world. The commercially exploited species are mainly the middle-sized ones, though some small species are sometimes eaten alive in Japan. These do not, as far as I know, include the blue-ringed octopus!

The three or four known blue-ringed octopuses are all species of the genus *Hapalochlaena*, living in tide pools, and sometimes in swimming pools (only salt-water ones, of course), in the western Pacific from Japan in the north to Australia in the south. Although only about 4-5cm (1½–2in) long, they are considered among the most venomous creatures on earth. Their normal prey is shrimps, crabs and small fish, but they will bite more or less anything, including humans, if provoked or even accidentally trodden on. The venom is a neurotoxin causing paralysis and respiratory arrest, often leading to death. There is no known antidote so, as in the case of the sea wasps (see Q7), I would recommend staying away from them!

12 Can squid fly?

Well, yes, they can actually. At least, some species can glide over the sea surface, using lift provided by their outstretched fins, in much the same way that flying fish can.

I have posed this question in the book's title because the answer came as a total surprise to me, despite having been a professional marine biologist throughout my working life. Until just a few years ago I was totally ignorant of flying squid, even though I worked with colleagues who were well aware of the phenomenon, and have a friendship of more than 40 years with one of the United States' foremost squid authorities.

This glaring hole in my knowledge was filled during a passage across the Indian Ocean from Fremantle to Reunion in February 2008. Along with my wife, I spent many hours on deck trying to get decent pictures of the many flying fish shoals we encountered. Anyone who has tried to do this will know how frustrating it is. First, you have no idea when the next fish will suddenly appear, nor exactly where it will emerge through the surface. And a bit like proverbial London buses, flying fish tend to occur in big groups (see Fig 10) separated by long periods of absolutely nothing. But once they appear, at least some individuals will stay out of the water for between five and ten seconds and 'fly' maybe a hundred metres or more. With this sort of window, even a ham-fisted amateur photographer like me has a fair chance of getting a reasonable photo (see Fig 11).

But from time to time I kept seeing another sort of 'flying fish' that stayed aloft for only a couple of seconds and moved no more than 5 or 10m (16–33ft) before splashing down into the sea. We came across the same phenomenon several times as we crossed the Indian Ocean and then again, after we had rounded South Africa, as we sailed through the subtropical Atlantic. My eyesight was not acute enough to resolve them properly, but as I concentrated on looking for and at them they appeared to be like white-ish flying capital letter 'I's, with a narrow central stem and somewhat wider bits at the front and back ends. And if the sun caught them at the right angle they could look like 15cm (6in) diameter bubbles or big glass Christmas tree decorations. Then I noticed that, as they left the water, many of them seemed to be dragging thin strings behind them, a bit like a kite on the end of its line. These 'strings' soon disappeared however, and for the remainder of the short flight the letter 'I's were totally disconnected from the water.

Gradually, it began to dawn on me what I was looking at, but it wasn't until I caught them on my camera that I could be certain. It took a long time. At first, the best I could get was a few images of very blurred 'I's, with or without the trailing string. But gradually I got a bit better at it and eventually obtained a few pictures like Fig 12, showing conclusively that these were, indeed, flying squid, with the cross pieces on my imagined letter 'I's being the outspread fins in front and the animals' tentacles behind. This also meant that the 'strings' were actually jets of water that the animals were using to launch themselves through the surface into their glide.

Squid can swim quite effectively, albeit reasonably slowly, using only their fins

Figure 10
A squadron of flying fish takes to the air in the South Atlantic.

Figure 11
A 'monoplane' Indian Ocean flying fish (probably a species of the genus *Exocoetus*) photographed south of Reunion Island. Some flying fish species have both the pectoral and pelvic fins enlarged to form a sort of 'biplane'.

Figure 12
Flying squid (probably *Sthenoteuthis pteropus*) photographed in the southern Atlantic Ocean in March 2008. It is 'flying' fins first towards the top of the picture and the two white dots just above the tentacles are the animal's eyes.

for propulsion. But if they want to move very rapidly, either tentacles first in order to catch a prey organism, or fins first to escape from a potential predator, they rapidly contract their muscles around the mantle cavity, a water-filled pouch close to the head end that also encloses their gills. The result is a narrow water jet a bit like the current of air we produce when we blow out a candle. In the squid's case, the jet can be directed forwards or backwards through a flexible funnel called a siphon. When it is under water, the squid can take in another mantle cavity-full of water and produce another jet, just as we can breathe in and fill our lungs before blowing out another candle. But having left the water, the flying squid has run out of fuel, so to speak, because it can't recharge its mantle cavity until it has dropped back into the sea. Consequently, unlike the flying fish, the squid can't have a second bite of the cherry by giving its forward momentum another boost while it is still in the air. So flying squid flights are generally much shorter, both in duration and distance, than those of flying fish.

When I sent my flying squid pictures to my old friend Dr Clyde Roper, ex squid expert of the United States Smithsonian Institution in Washington, he became quite excited, suggesting that my photos were among the best available. Apparently, the squid could belong to any number of small, surface-dwelling species known to indulge in this behaviour to escape from predators. However, based on his knowledge of squid distribution, as well as a few clues from the photos themselves, Clyde suggests that they were probably the orange-back squid, *Sthenoteuthis pteropus*[21]; that's good enough for me!

13 Why do you find turtles wandering around in the open ocean?

Apart from whales, dolphins, seabirds and flying fish, the most commonly seen vertebrate creatures at the surface of the open sea are probably turtles, particularly in the warmer waters of the world ocean. They are almost always seen singly, wandering along rather aimlessly, often hundreds of miles from the nearest land. So what on earth are they doing there? Well, basically they are doing what most animals do most of the time – looking for something to eat, trying to avoid being eaten and hoping to come across a potential mate! And in the case of mature female turtles, they are often migrating to or from the beaches where they lay their eggs because, although they spend most of their time at sea, all female turtles have to come back to land to breed. There are several dozens of well-known sandy turtle-breeding beaches scattered around the world ocean. Some are on continental land masses like North and South America, Africa and Australia and on large islands in the Caribbean and the Indo-Pacific, but many are on remote oceanic islands such as Ascension Island in the Atlantic, used by green turtles that regularly migrate to the coast of South America to feed. Each female lays up to about 100 eggs at a time and buries them beneath the sand. A female may make several such egg-laying visits to the beach during a single breeding season, depositing several hundred eggs. The eggs are left unattended and the tiny turtle babies hatch after six to eight weeks into a hostile and dangerous world.

Marine turtles are reptiles, belonging to the same group that contains the snakes, lizards, crocodiles and alligators. But their nearest relatives are the terrestrial tortoises and the freshwater terrapins and turtles. The limbs of the marine species are modified to become efficient paddles but, as a result, are not very good for walking across land surfaces. There are only seven recognised species of true marine turtles. Six of these, the green, hawksbill, loggerhead, flatback, Kemp's

---

21   Meaning 'winged narrow squid'. When the squid was described in 1855 by the Danish biologist Japetus
      Steenstrup, he presumably gave it the 'winged' bit of its Latin name because he knew it could 'fly'.
      Since I had been well aware of its scientific name for many years, my failure to realise it was a flyer
      was even more remiss!

ridley and olive ridley, have hard shells like their land-based relatives and grow up to half a metre to a metre (1½–3ft) or so long. Several of them are very widespread, with the commonest, the green turtle, being found in all the tropical and subtropical waters of the world, though two distinct forms are recognised, one in the Atlantic/Mediterranean and one in the Indo-Pacific. The seventh marine turtle species, the leathery or leatherback turtle, has a soft leather-like shell, as its name suggests. It is by far the biggest species, reaching a length of almost 2m (6ft) and weighing up to 500kg (1,102lb) or more. Like the other marine turtles, the leatherback is most common in warm waters, but it also wanders into quite cold areas, being recorded in the Atlantic from northern Norway to south of the Cape of Good Hope. It also seems to dive deeper than the other species in search of food, being said to reach depths of 1,000m (3,280ft) or more, whereas the other marine turtles probably go no deeper than a few tens of metres and stay submerged for only five to ten minutes.

Adult green turtles are herbivores, feeding mainly on seagrasses in relatively shallow water. However, juvenile green turtles eat almost anything they can find, and most adult marine turtles are carnivores, feeding on fish, crustaceans, molluscs, sponges and, particularly in the open sea, jellyfish (see Q6).

Adult marine turtles have few natural enemies apart from man, because their size and their tough shells protect them from anything but the biggest and most voracious fish and whales. However, in the past the marine turtles were extensively hunted for food, for their shells or for use in medicines. Some of them still are, so that several species are considered to be endangered and are protected in many parts of the world. Since they all bury their eggs on sandy shores, the tiny turtles are particularly vulnerable to natural predators such as seabirds, reptiles, seals and even coastal mammals as they dig their way out of the nest and crawl down to the water's edge. Some of the nesting sites are visited by so many turtles that they have become major tourist attractions. Unfortunately, unless the visits are carefully managed, the potential disturbance adds yet another pressure on the animals' survival.

14 Could the story of Jonah and the whale be true?

In a word, no! But let's see why not.

According to the book of Jonah in the Bible, the prophet was ordered by the Lord to go to Nineveh, near the modern city of Mosul in Iraq, to chastise it because, said the Lord, its citizens had turned to wickedness. But Jonah didn't fancy the job and decided to do a runner by taking a ship from Joppa, the modern port of Jaffa to the south of Tel Aviv, Israel, heading for a place called Tarshish. Nobody seems to know where, exactly, Tarshish was or is, except that it was a long way away from Joppa. Far enough, hoped Jonah, for him to escape the wrath of the Lord. But he was wrong.

Once Jonah's ship was out at sea the Lord sent a 'great wind', raising huge seas that threatened to sink the vessel. Realising that it was all his fault, Jonah told the sailors to throw him overboard, after which the Lord would calm the seas. Reluctant at first, the sailors eventually did as Jonah said – and, sure enough, the seas calmed down. We are not told what happened to the ship; presumably it either sailed on to Tarshish or went back to Joppa. Either way, the action stayed with Jonah who, instead of drowning, was swallowed by 'a great fish' thoughtfully provided by the Lord. Perhaps not surprisingly, inside this unexpected saviour Jonah repented. After three days the Lord arranged for the great fish to spew him up onto dry land and, again not too surprisingly, Jonah did as he was told the next time the Lord suggested that he should go to Nineveh.

So what are we to make of this story, apart from the obvious religious aspects of it? Although whales get mentioned specifically elsewhere in the Bible, the term is never used in relation to Jonah. Nevertheless, in popular culture the story has come down to us as 'Jonah and the whale' – and for good reason. After all, there aren't many beasts in the ocean remotely big enough to swallow a man whole, even a small one! And most of those that are big enough are whales.

But irrespective of which beast's stomach Jonah might or might not have found himself in, let's first look at how long he might have survived in it. The answer is, of course, a few minutes at most! The inside of any animal's stomach is a pretty nasty environment for any form of life other than the specialised bacteria or gut parasites that routinely make a living there. For one thing, it is often slewing in corrosive digestive juices and a pretty disgusting soup made up of recently ingested food in varying states of decomposition. But as if this wouldn't be bad enough, the real killer for an air-breathing mammal like Jonah is the total absence of breathable air. So Jonah's survival would be absolutely dependent upon how long he could hold his breath, after which he would drown in an indescribably appalling manner that doesn't bear thinking about. So how long might that be?

As a kid I remember my dad teaching me the old rule-of-thumb adage that a human can survive only three minutes without air, three days without water and three weeks without food. There are quite a few records of people being success- fully resuscitated after total immersion for considerably longer than three minutes in very cold water. But under most circumstances the three-minute limit is not far out, and most of us would have some difficulty holding our breath even for that fairly short length of time.

There are, of course, lots of diving specialists and other enthusiasts who can hold their breath considerably longer than this. For example, in April 2010, as I was writing this piece, news came through that several records had been broken at this year's Vertical Blue diving competition held at Dean's Blue Hole in the Bahamas. Perhaps the most remarkable feat was the Constant Weight No Fins (or CNF) record broken by New Zealander William Trubridge. As the title indicates, in this strange event the participant must swim down a line simply holding his or her breath, without using fins, and come back to the surface with a tag collected at the bottom of the dive and proving the greatest depth attained. Trubridge reached an amazing depth of 92m (301ft), returning to the surface after an immersion of 3 minutes and 45 seconds – and then proceeded to beat his own record by reaching 95m (311ft) a few days later. As if this wasn't enough, Trubridge then went on to achieve another record, this time reaching a depth of 116m (380ft) in the Free Immersion (FIM) event. In this so-called sport, the competitor must again reach the greatest possible depth with a single breath and without swimming aids like fins, but this time able to pull himself down using the rope. Apart from being a mind-blowing feat, the important point from the Jonah argument point of view is that Trubridge held his breath for a full 4 minutes and 9 seconds.

But these seemingly awesome results pale into insignificance beside the world record for breath-holding, established by the magician-cum-publicity stuntman David Blaine in April 2008 as an astonishing 17 minutes and 4 seconds. Whatever you think of some of his antics, few would deny that Blaine has some remarkable talents. But even he had to prepare very carefully to achieve the record, which still falls well short of Jonah's three-day breath-holding feat accomplished immediately after being thrown overboard from a violently moving ship! So unless Jonah had some breath-holding abilities unequalled by any human before or since, mercifully the whole ghastly business would have been over in a matter of minutes and the story is totally impossible.

Amazingly, despite the obvious incredibility of Jonah-like stories, we humans seem fascinated by these ghoulish ideas and most cultures have folk tales based on human survival after being swallowed by some beast or other. And sometimes, like urban myths, they can be told with a remarkable degree of conviction. In his excellent book *Leviathan*, published by Fourth Estate in 2008, Philip Hoare refers to a number of published accounts purporting to document humans swallowed by whales. One of the most graphic of these, and probably the most frequently repeated, concerns a sailor on a whaling ship, the *Star of the East*, working off the Falkland Islands in 1891. According to at least one of the accounts, the sailor, James Bartley, was in one of two whaling boats pursuing a large sperm whale and was thrown into the water after his boat was attacked and destroyed by the harpooned whale. The animal was eventually killed and when its carcass was being cut up some 36 hours later Bartley was found curled up in the stomach, unconscious but alive. After a bath in seawater and two weeks' care to get over a period as 'a raving lunatic', he apparently recovered more or less completely apart from some discoloration of his skin from the whale's digestive juices.

Although Hoare simply passes over this story with a rather cynical nod and wink, he does not dissect it in any great detail. However, the affair has been examined very thoroughly and is the subject of an article 'A Whale of a Tale: Fundamentalist Fish Stories', published by Edward B. Davis in *Perspectives on Science and Christian Faith* 43: 224–237, 1991. In this very well researched article, the author comes to the conclusion that there is not a shred of truth in the story, not least because there was no one on the *Star of the East* at the time with a name remotely like James Bartley, there was no whale caught by the vessel off the Falklands (or anywhere else for that matter because the ship was not a whaler) and, perhaps most telling of all, in later years the captain's wife, who had accompanied her husband throughout the period in question, denied all knowledge of the event. Although Davis admits that we will probably never know how the story arose in the first place, he suggests that it possibly began as a hoax to extract money from a sensation-hungry public and was subsequently embraced by Christian fundamentalists as evidence in support of a fondly held Bible story.

But let's get back to Jonah and be even more pedantic by looking for any marine creature with a stomach that he could possibly have managed to get himself into in one piece. First, let's look at the non-whale contenders.

Basically we are talking about the three biggest shark species – the whale shark, the basking shark and the great white shark. The two biggest, the whale shark at possibly up to 15–20m (50–65ft) long and the basking shark at up to 12m (40ft) long, are both plankton feeders, consistently swimming close to the surface with their mouths wide open to filter from the water tiny food particles mostly no more than a few centimetres long. Under no circumstances would they voluntarily attack, far less swallow, a human. And if they did manage to swallow a person in some strange accident the outcome would be just as fatal for the shark as for the human, so they can certainly be excluded from auditions for the role of Jonah's 'great fish'.

But what about the great white shark, the infamous subject of Peter Benchley's novel made into the blockbuster film *Jaws* by Steven Spielberg in 1975? Is this a possible contender? Well, compared with the whale shark and basking shark in terms of size alone, the great white is a mere tiddler at a maximum length of no more than about 6m (20ft) or so. But unlike its big brothers, the great white is a notoriously voracious predator, feeding on large fish, squid, seals and small dolphins

– and it is undoubtedly a potential maneater! On the other hand, despite its terrible reputation, great white attacks on humans are very, very rare, considering the numbers of sharks in the seas and the numbers of humans swimming in waters frequented by them. Furthermore, even when such attacks do occur they are by no means always fatal. For example, only a small number of the 31 confirmed attacks on humans over the last two centuries in the Mediterranean, the location of Jonah's adventure, resulted in death. And in not a single case was the victim swallowed whole. Indeed, the cause of death was precisely because the attacking shark was *not* trying to swallow its prey in one piece but, instead, was attempting to remove a more manageable lump like a leg, an arm or a thigh – hence the horrific injuries typically resulting from great white attacks. Consequently, if any or all of the prophet had ended up in the tummy of a great white it would have been in bite-sized pieces not at all suitable for vomiting up reassembled. Bang goes the possibility of 'Jaws' being Jonah's 'whale'.

Now let's look at the whales themselves as possible Jonah swallowers[22]. Biologists have divided the 80 or so species of whales and dolphins into two main divisions, the whalebone whales and the toothed whales. The whalebone whales (or Mysticetes[23]) contains all those species that feed on relatively small food particles by filtering the water through a sort of sieve formed by the bristly edges of a series of plates of horny baleen or 'whalebone' (hence the name) hanging down on either side of the upper jaw. But although all whalebone whales make a living by feeding on fairly small stuff, they use one or other of two quite distinct feeding techniques. One lot, the right whales or bowhead whales, have huge heads making up almost one third of the total body length and very large mouths equipped with hundreds of 2–4m (6–13ft) long baleen plates. These whales all swim slowly near the surface with their mouths wide open so that water can enter the front of the mouth and leave on either side towards the back of the gape, having been sieved through the baleen plates[24]. Any small food items, mainly

---

22   For help at this point I went to an old friend and work colleague, Dr Howard Roe. I've known Howard for more than 40 years and for the last few years of my working life he was my boss as Director of the Southampton Oceanography Centre, where I worked. More relevantly, however, Howard had had a quite remarkable scientific career. For many years before he went into scientific administration, Howard studied some of the smallest creatures in the marine plankton, the copepods – little shrimp-like creatures that occur in such huge numbers in the oceans that they are major constituents of the diets of lots of much bigger beasts, including some of the huge plankton-feeding animals like the whalebone whales. And amazingly, Howard had spent the early years of his scientific life working on these very leviathans. Consequently, he has stared down the throats, and sifted through the stomach contents, of more big whales than anyone I know. Who better to tell me whether or not Jonah could have found his way into one of their tummies!

23   Meaning 'moustached' whales, from the Greek word 'mystax' meaning moustache, and referring to the baleen or whalebone plates inside the mouths of these whales.

24   This feeding technique is very similar to that used by the whale shark and the basking shark, which also live on small food particles.

copepods and other small crustaceans, are retained on the inner surfaces of the baleen plates and are periodically 'licked' off by the enormous tongue and pushed into the back of the throat and swallowed. The gape of these beasts is certainly big enough to accommodate a Jonah, though their slow swimming speeds, like those of the basking shark and whale shark, make them extremely unlikely Jonah swallowers.

Figure 13
Young male humpback, about 11m (36ft) long, throwing himself out of the water at Icy Strait, Alaska, apparently simply full of *joie de vivre*!

So what about the other lot of moustached or whalebone whales, the rorquals? These are the half a dozen really big whales ranging from the minke, at about 10m (33ft) long and weighing around 25 tonnes, through most people's favourite, the humpback, up to 15m (50ft) and over 30 tonnes (see Fig 13), to the huge blue whale at up to 33m (108ft) long and weighing as much as 190 tonnes. Like the right whales, the rorquals filter relatively small food particles out of the water using their baleen plates, but unlike the right whales, rorquals swim quite fast and periodically take in huge gulps of water from which they sieve out whatever it contained, often including fairly big and fast-swimming fish. To enable them to make a living with this feeding technique, the rorquals are able to enlarge the volume of their mouth cavity enormously by opening out the throat grooves or skin folds extending from the lower jaw to behind the flippers in all species[25]. As my personal whale expert (see [22]) pointed out, 'in a big fin whale of, say, 70 foot long, this would be a balloon around 10 foot or so across since the lower jaw of such a beast would be 7–8ft across'. So there would be plenty of room for a quite big Jonah in the mouth cavity of a big rorqual. And because they swim so fast it seems at least possible that, albeit inadvertently, a rorqual might take in a man-sized lump. But what would it do with such an embarrassment of riches? Well, according to my informant, not much! To quote his words, 'The actual throat [of big rorquals] is about 10 inches across and apparently doesn't stretch – so Jonah would not get far!' So we seem to have drawn a blank yet again.

Figure 14
Two typical toothed whales, a common dolphin (photographed in the western North Atlantic) and a bottlenose dolphin (photographed off Ascension Island).

Finally, we are left with the toothed whales or Odontocetes. These include all the really fast-swimming cetaceans such as the porpoises and dolphins, which feed on equally fast-swimming prey like fish and squid. But most of these whales are far too small to be even vaguely considered as potential Jonah swallowers. The very biggest dolphin, the 10m (33ft) long killer whale or orca, is quite capable of killing a human, as the world was tragically reminded in February 2010 when animal trainer Dawn Brancheau was grabbed and drowned by a bull orca in the SeaWorld amusement park in Orlando, Florida[26]. In the wild, of course, orcas are well known to be voracious predators on fish, squid, seals and even other whales. Most of us have seen the amazing films of orcas attacking tight shoals of herring-sized fish and

---

25   As *Do Whales...?* pointed out, the name 'rorqual' is derived from the Norwegian word *rorhval*, meaning 'grooved whale'.
26   Though it didn't try to eat her, of course.

apparently eating them more or less whole. But we have also seen the distressing images of killer whales apparently 'playing' with seals rather like cats play with mice, and ganging up on whale calves, particularly those of gray whales in the Pacific. And all these cases involve the spilling of a lot of blood as the unfortunate prey are torn to pieces, for the orcas are clearly unable to swallow individual morsels bigger than, say, a leg of lamb. So we still haven't found a Jonah swallower and we are down to our very last contender, the sperm whale.

The sperm whale, *Physeter macrocephalus,* also known as the cachalot, and the eponymous object of Herman Melville's *Moby Dick,* is the largest of all the toothed whales. Although the largest sperm whales are much smaller than the really big rorquals, they are still impressive beasts. Female sperm whales are relatively tiddly, growing no bigger than about 12m (40ft) long. But the males, or bulls, can reach a pretty impressive length of 18m (60ft). With a strange squarish head, typically occupying almost one third of the total body length, you might think there would be plenty of room for an enormous mouth and jaw. And the sperm whale mouth is, indeed, rather impressive, but it is not quite as big as you would think.

From the general appearance of a sperm whale's head you might expect that the skull and its associated bits and pieces, including the jaw, would be similarly massive and squarish. But you would be wrong. In fact, the bulk of the head, the huge square forehead, is completely outside the animal's skull and is occupied by a massive cavity, the melon, filled with a waxy substance called spermaceti[27].

The skull itself is relatively small by whale standards, but the upper and lower jaw, extending forwards from the lower part of the skull underneath the melon, is impressively long, up to about 2m (6–7ft) in a big bull. And the teeth are amazing too, with bulls having as many as 25 or 26 pairs up to 25cm (10in) long, while in females they are rather fewer and smaller. But neither sex has functional teeth in the upper jaw, and some adults have been caught – apparently in good condition and not starving – with hardly any teeth at all. This has led some whale experts to suggest that the teeth may not be very important in normal feeding but, instead, may play a part in competition between males. In any case, despite the size of the teeth and the length of the jaw, the total volume of a sperm whale's mouth is pretty puny because the width between the rows of teeth is no more than about half a metre (20in). Nevertheless, sperm whales swallow man-sized giant squid whole, somehow squeezing the somewhat rubbery skeleton-less body through a 25cm (10in) or so diameter throat. So while a determined and fairly narrow-shouldered Jonah, suitably lined up, might just about make it into a sperm whale tummy, as my whale-savvy pal put it, 'I strongly suspect that he might have got squashed a bit going down!'

---

27   In *'Do Whales...?'* I explained how this term became applied to the material because of the strange and rather ridiculous belief of early whalers that it was sperm!

So there you have it – or almost. As I finished this section, in July 2010, the scientific journal *Nature* published an account of the discovery in Peru of the fossilised skeletal remains of a giant prehistoric ancestral sperm whale. This long-disappeared beast, apparently to be named *Leviathan mellvillei* in honour of Moby Dick's creator, is thought to have lived some 12 million years ago. It seems to have been about the same overall size as a modern sperm whale, that is reaching a total length approaching 18m (60ft), but its head and jaws seem to have been relatively much bigger. Whereas modern sperm whales have teeth only in the lower jaw, the Peruvian beast had lots of teeth in both the upper and lower jaws, and what teeth they were! As I've pointed out, modern sperm whale teeth are pretty impressive, weighing up to a kilogram and reaching a length approaching 25cm (8–10in), but the teeth in the fossil are absolutely massive, up to 35cm (14in) long and much chunkier than their modern relatives. They were clearly not just for show and the palaeontologists reporting the find are speculating that their beast had a similar role to the present day killer whale. But they believe that *Leviathan* was much more powerful, being able to take on the very biggest beast in their contemporary seas and possibly capable of swallowing huge lumps. However, as a contender for the role of Jonah swallower, it was about 11¾ million years too early!

15 Where does the name 'whale' come from?

The terms *whale* in English, *Wal* or *Walfisch* in German and *hval* in the Scandinavian languages are all derived from the Anglo-Saxon word *hwael*, meaning wheel. It presumably originally referred to the resemblance of a surfacing whale to a revolving submerged wheel.

16 Do all whales live in the sea?

It depends what you mean by 'whales'. The group Cetacea, to which the whales belong, contains about 80 different species ranging from the huge blue whale to some small dolphins and porpoises only about a metre or so long when they are fully grown. Although what we refer to as 'whales' are generally bigger than dolphins, there is a gradation in size between the smallest dolphins and the largest whales, with no clear gap between them. In fact, the biggest dolphin, the killer whale or orca, clearly deserves the name 'whale', so that the names dolphin and whale are not mutually exclusive.

All the very biggest whales, and certainly the plankton-feeding whalebone whales, are totally confined to the sea, not least of all because they simply could not find enough food to survive in rivers and lakes.

Many coastal-living toothed whales and dolphins, on the other hand, enter rivers from time to time and may regularly penetrate long distances into the freshwater realm. For example, the tucuxi (pronounced 'tookooshee'), a small (less than 2m/7ft long) dolphin of the Atlantic coastal waters of South America, penetrates more than 250 kilometres (155 miles) up the Orinoco River and 2,500km (1,500 miles) up the Amazon.

Finally, some of the largest and muddiest rivers of South America and Asia have their own very specialised river dolphins, the pink dolphin or boto of the Amazon and Orinoco, the baiji or Yangtze River dolphin (possibly now extinct), and the Indus and Ganges River dolphins. The river dolphins share a number of adaptations to their very specific environments. They all have poor or non-existent eyesight and instead rely on echo-location, a bit like bats, to 'visualise' their surroundings. They all have long thin beaks that are presumably specialised for catching freshwater fish and invertebrates. They all dive for rather short periods, rarely more than a minute or so, and they are all rather slow-moving and shy, and therefore difficult to see.

So if you rephrase the question to ask if all Cetaceans live in the sea, the answer is definitely no! But most species, and certainly the larger ones, certainly prefer the marine environment. Unfortunately, from time to time odd individuals of normally totally marine species make a wrong turn and end up in rivers, often with tragic results. Many people will remember the news coverage of the northern bottlenose whale that wandered into the River Thames as far as central London in the summer of 2006. Almost inevitably, the story had a sad ending when the whale died during the rescue operation attempting to return it to its proper environment.

17 How long do whales live – and how do we know?

In general, as with many animal groups, the larger the species, the longer it will live. For example, among the toothed whales or Odontocetes, harbour porpoises (less than 2m/7ft long) are thought to live for about 15 years, the bottlenose dolphin (up to about 4m/13ft long) for about 25 years, the white whale or beluga (up to 5m/16ft long) for 25–30 years, the northern bottlenose whale (up to 9m/30ft long) for up to 37 years, the killer whale (up to about 10m/33ft long) for 50+ years in the male and 80+ years in the female, short-finned pilot whales (up to 7m/23ft long) for up to 63 years, sperm whale (up to 18m/59ft long) for 65–70 years and Baird's beaked whale (up to almost 13m/43ft long) for up to 70 years. Whalebone whales are also long-lived. For example, humpback whales (up to 15m/49ft long) live at least 30 years, minke whales (up to 10m/33ft long) for 40–50 years, sei whales (up to 16m/53ft long) to 65 years and fin whales (up to 22m/72ft long) for 85–90 years. Blue whales, the largest of all (up to 27m/88ft long), are thought to have a life span about the same as fin whales, that is 80–90 years or so, much the same as we humans[28].

But just as some humans live much longer than most of us, reaching ages well over 100, the same seems to be true of whales, and there are some well-substantiated records of very old whales. Most of these are based on direct estimates of the age of dead whales from examination of bits of the body. In the toothed whales, which include all the small species such as the porpoises and dolphins, the animals can be aged by counting growth rings in the teeth, much as horses can be aged. But the baleen or whalebone whales have no hard teeth. Instead, they have horny whalebone filters hanging inside their mouths to capture their food. For many years these big whales were aged by measuring variations in thickness of the whalebone, thought to be more or less equivalent to the annual growth rings in trees. But this technique is both difficult and of questionable reliability, so in the middle years of the 20th century whale biologists were very anxious to find a better method. It eventually arrived in the unassuming form of a rather nasty-looking waxy plug from deep inside whales' ears!

In the interests of streamlining, whales don't have external ears sticking out of their bodies like most land mammals do, including us humans. But otherwise their ears are basically pretty much like ours. They have an external auditory meatus, the ear canal, open to the water at one end and leading to the tympanic membrane, and thence to the inner ear, at the other. But because sound transmission through water is rather different from through air, whale ears have a number of special characteristics, one of which is to have the inner end of the ear canal filled with a waxy lump, the ear plug, which seems to be particularly efficient at transmitting the incoming sounds to the membrane. As the whale's skull grows, so does the ear canal – and with it, the plug. Biologists studying the auditory anatomy of whales at the Natural History Museum in London in the 1950s realised that annular marks seen in cross sections of the plugs when they were cut in half might be growth rings, just like those in trees or teeth.

After a few years of trial and uncertainty this conclusion proved to be correct, so during the last half-century ear-plug analysis has been the main technique for aging whalebone whales. However, as the animals get older, growth of the ear plug becomes slower and slower; thus it becomes increasingly difficult to count

28   These figures are taken from *Whales and Dolphins*, by Peter GH Evans, published in 1987 by Academic Press, where details of the original references are given.

them, so that aging very old whales is a bit of a problem. Occasionally, quite unexpected evidence may come to the rescue as it did in 2007 when native Inuit hunters caught a bowhead whale off the coast of Alaska. When the carcass of the unfortunate individual was being cut up, a 13cm long (5in) fragment of an ancient harpoon was found embedded in its flesh. Amazingly, the weapon was identified as having been made at a New England factory in about 1880 and must have been used within the subsequent few years. This suggested the intriguing likelihood that the whale had been unsuccessfully hunted well over a century ago and had carried the remains of the weapon used ever since. The whale would certainly already have been large when hunted the first time, with the implication that when killed it might easily have been well over 150 years old!

18 What is the difference between seals and sea lions?

Seals and sea lions belong to a rather small group of mammals called the Pinnipedia, a name made up of two Latin words together meaning 'feather or wing footed'. The pinnipeds contain about 20 living species including, apart from the seals and sea lions, the fur seals and the walrus. Zoologists divide the group into two main subdivisions, one, the 'eared seals', containing the sea lions, fur seals and walrus, and the other, the true or 'earless seals' (see Fig 15). There are lots of detailed internal differences between them, but Fig 15 illustrates the obvious

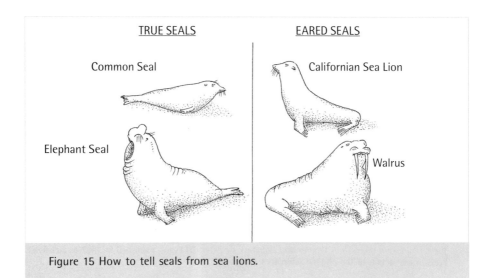

Figure 15 How to tell seals from sea lions.

external differences which also separate seals and sea lions. The simple answer to the question is that in true seals the rear flippers point backwards and cannot be bent forwards beneath the body. Consequently, although they are superb swimmers, on land the true seals cannot take the full weight of their bodies on their fins and have to move by wriggling movements. In contrast, the eared seals, including the sea lions, fur seals and walrus, have hind flippers that can be turned forwards under the body, enabling them to walk quite effectively on land, albeit with a somewhat waddling gait. Apart from the walrus, eared seals, as the name suggests, have external ears, a bit like ours but only 2–3cm (1in) long, so they are often quite difficult to spot (see Figs 16 and 17).

Figure 16
South African fur seal in Capetown Harbour. Note the small, but obvious, external ears.

Figure 17
Harbour seal at Bergen Aquarium. An obvious earhole, but no external ear.

II
Edible Marine Biology

This section was prompted by the realisation that lots of us have only the vaguest idea of what we are eating, whether it is something included in a restaurant or gastro-pub menu or presented to us in clingfilm-wrapped sterility by a supermarket.

When I was a youngster, more years ago than I care to remember, the local fish-monger would have a reasonably comprehensive knowledge of what he was selling. This was not too surprising because, with rare exceptions, he (or she) would be selling pretty unremarkable local stuff, no more than a couple of dozen species of fish ranging from salmon and trout at the top end, through the middle latitudes, so to speak, of cod, pollack, hake and haddock, via half a dozen flatfish like plaice, flounder, sole, halibut and the slightly exotic skate, to the pretty mundane herring, sprats, pilchards and whitebait and some inexplicably cheap and fairly nondescript stuff called huss or rock salmon. From time to time the inland fishmonger might carry a 'special' like ling or John Dory. But certainly in Northamptonshire where I was brought up and, I suspect, in many other areas, these exotics were exactly that – exotic, and therefore both pretty unusual and far too expensive for most people to contemplate.

The same applied to the other staple area of the fishmonger's wares, the shell-fish, the crustaceans and molluscs that graced his stall. The top end of this lot (at least as far as cost was concerned) were undoubtedly the lobsters among the crustaceans and the oysters among the molluscs. Then you could move down through the crustaceans via crabs, or rather *crab* because there was only one species sold in most fishmongers, to the prawns, almost always sold pre-boiled, and finally to the smaller shrimps, also either boiled or 'potted' in small glass jars and topped up with melted butter. Moving to the molluscs, if you were really posh you might aspire to a few oysters, always sold alive and traditionally then, as now, eaten in the same state. But beyond the oysters you might go for much more homely and cheaper options. These would include cockles and mussels, like oysters usually sold 'alive alive oh' (as did poor Molly Malone until the fever got her, according to the Irish song), and then to the cheapest end of the market represented by whelks and winkles. But you would rarely see scallops on the slab because these were generally thought of as far too exotic and/or expensive for normal British taste. And although I am pretty sure that squid appeared from time to time on my local Mac Fisheries slab, I can't remember ever having seen them.

So that was just about it. No more than about 30 marine creatures routinely offered for sale by most inland fishmongers, with perhaps another 10 or 15 species offered in coastal towns or the better stores in big cities. And virtually all of them would have been caught in British waters, or at least landed in British ports.

But much of what was landed here was never offered to the British consumer – mainly, I fear, because he or she didn't want it or wouldn't have been prepared to pay a decent price for it. For example – and it seems amazing to me now – I rarely, if ever, saw scampi on the fishmonger's slab, and had it been there it would probably have been called Dublin Bay prawn because the word 'scampi', as far as the Brits were concerned, had not yet been invented[29]! And when I was a PhD student in Port Erin on the Isle of Man in the 1960s there was a thriving scallop fishery but, with very rare exceptions, the catches were always bagged up into hessian sacks and shipped off to London and mostly, thereafter, to the Continent, where they commanded a much higher price than at home.

How different things are nowadays, when my local Sainsburys routinely offers squid tubes from India, prawns from the Philippines, queen scallops from Patagonia, king scallops from North America or Canada, green-lipped mussels from New Zealand, basa fillets from goodness knows where and much, much more; a veritable confusion of riches. And with the best will in the world, the person serving you behind the counter can't be expected to know the ins and outs of all these exotics – any more than I did before I started to put this section together. So what follows is simply my attempt to de-mystify this situation a little by explaining what some of the creatures on the fish counter are, where they come from and, in some cases, a bit of information about how they live.

19 What are scallops?

Scallops (pronounced with the first syllable rhyming with either 'pal' or 'doll')[30] are bivalve molluscs, belonging to the same group that contains the oysters, mussels

29   And 'scampi' now seems to have been replaced by the term 'langoustine'.
30   The Oxford English Dictionary, the acknowledged arbiter in all things appertaining to the English language, at least on the eastern side of the Atlantic, says that scallop is 'usually pronounced' as if it rhymes with dollop. But it doesn't come to a definitive decision one way or the other. So it seems to me that you can please yourself whether you pronounce it 'skallop' or 'skollop'; who cares!

and clams. Scallops belong to the family Pectenidae, so-called because their rounded shells with radiating ribs vaguely resemble the traditional Roman comb, for which the Latin word is *pecten*[31]. In Europe the name is applied particularly to the great scallop, *Pecten maximus,* but worldwide it can be used for about two hundred very similar species found in warm and temperate seas, many of which are commercially exploited.

Scallops have been fished seriously in European waters for many decades, though the landings increased very substantially from the 1970s onwards. These fisheries are still very important locally; for example, in 2007 the Scottish scallop fishery landed some 8,800 tonnes, worth more than £18 million. However, on a global scale the European fisheries are dwarfed by those for the western Atlantic species, *Placopecten magellanicus,* caught off the eastern United States and Canada, and the Pacific scallop, *Patinopecten yessoensis,* fished particularly around China and Japan. Most of these commercially exploited scallops are collected from the wild using dredges or trawls, or in some areas by divers. However, there is also a considerable scallop-farming industry, originating in Japan in the 1970s and based initially on *Patinopecten yessoensis,* but now practised in many parts of the world with the local species, including the European scallop, *Pecten maximus.*

Scallops come in two fairly distinct size categories, the smaller ones usually called queen scallops or queenies, and the bigger ones sometimes distinguished as king scallops. All the species referred to above are king scallops. By the time they are saleable these have shells usually 10–15cm (4–5in) wide, whereas queen scallops are only 7–8cm (3in) wide. Queens are not simply young members of the king scallop species, but are separate species, mostly belonging to the genus *Chlamys* and its close relatives. In fact, one of the biggest scallop fisheries in the world, for the Patagonian scallop and producing about 45,000 tonnes a year, is actually for a queen scallop, *Zygochlamys patagonica.*

Naturally, the edible bits of king scallops are much bigger than those of queens – you get about 20–35 king scallop muscles per kilogram, compared with 40–100 or more for queens. In the shell they are even easier to distinguish, because whereas queen scallops have both shells curved, king scallops have one shell curved and one flat (see below). The curved shell is the one used to serve the scallop 'on the half shell'; it was also used frequently in the past as an ashtray in seaside pubs and restaurants.

Whereas we humans routinely eat the entire contents of the shells of mussels, cockles and oysters, we are a bit selective when it comes to scallops. We generally eat only the so-called adductor muscle, the big white round lump that holds the

---

31 Accordingly, the Roman writer and natural historian Pliny the Elder used the term 'pecten' for both combs and scallops.

two shells together, and the gonads or roe, the curved bit that is orange at one end (the female part) and white or creamish at the other (the male part). These are often the only parts of the scallop offered for sale on the fishmonger's slab or the supermarket fish counter. But most of the rest of the scallop's body can also be eaten, being particularly useful in the preparation of sauces or soups. This consists of the mantle or skirt, which in life lines the inner surface of the shell, and the gills. If you are preparing the scallops from scratch (ie in the complete shell), try to remove all the dark bits and pieces lying between the muscle and the hinge, which basically make up the scallop's 'innards' including the gut and digestive gland, vaguely equivalent to our liver. But don't get paranoid about this; none of it will kill you!

And whatever you do with a scallop, don't overcook it. Whichever way you cook them (fried, grilled, boiled or whatever), scallop flesh will get tougher and tougher if you cook it for more than 3 or 4 minutes. And don't make it compete with other tastes – it will frequently lose. The natural taste of scallop flesh, and gonads, is fantastic but delicate. If you cover it with garlic, onion, cheese or, heaven forbid, curry or chilli, you will ruin the scallop. In my opinion, a little salt and pepper on a scallop fried for a couple of minutes in butter is perfect. But what do I know?

20 How did scallops get their name?

The inclusion of this question is all down to Wikipedia, the internet free encyclopedia. Like most people, although I am fascinated by the amount of information so easily available on Wikipedia, I am a bit leery of articles on topics I know nothing about because you clearly can't take all of it on trust. The Wikipedia article on scallops is a case in point. Amazingly, it attributes the origin of the name 'scallop' to the ancient Canaanite sea port of Ascalon, now the modern city of Ashkelon in Israel. But although Ascalon almost certainly gave us the names 'scallions' and 'shallots', the term scallop originated far away, in north-western Europe[32].

The true origins of scallop are in a word that would have sounded something like *Skal*, used by northern Germanic tribes more than 2,000 years ago to signify some sort of hard covering and eventually giving us our modern word 'shell' (*Schale*

---

32   In 1957 the Shell Transport and Trading Company celebrated its 60th anniversary. Since 1904 the company had used a scallop shell as its symbol, what we would now call its logo, though this word did not come into common use until much later. To mark the event, the company commissioned and published a lavishly produced book, *The Scallop: Studies of a shell and its influences on humankind*, with sections written by eminent authorities of the time. I have pinched much of its information for this item.

in German and *schelp* in Dutch). It probably took several hundreds of years before the word became applied more specifically to animal shells like those of crabs and snails, but by medieval times it had certainly become *scelpe* and was being applied to what we now call scallops. Indeed, the Oxford English Dictionary records the word 'scallop' used in its modern sense as early as 1440!

But whether this spelling arose directly from the earlier spelling or by a round-about route is debatable. One persuasive argument suggests that it was first exported into French, possibly soon after the Norman conquest, as *escalope* because the medieval French couldn't cope with *scelpe*'s clusters of consonants. They used this new word to describe all sorts of shellfish, presumably including the scallop, but also snail shells and even nut shells. But then it disappeared for a long, long time before it eventually reappeared in the mid 19th century to be used in a totally new sense as *'escalope de veau'* that is, escalope of veal. And that is essentially what 'escalope' means today in French; if you look the word up in a modern French dictionary, it will define it as 'a thin slice of white meat, especially veal'.

In the meantime, the word 'escalope' came back into English because the Royal court and nobles during the early middle ages switched frequently between English and French and often mixed the two languages. Inevitably, this mixture of languages spilled out to the ordinary English folk who, the story goes, mispronounced esca-lope as scallop – and the rest, as they say, is history.

But how did the term 'scallop' become attached to the creature we use it for today? Well, the clue to this is in what the French call the scallop now – *coquille Saint Jacques*, that is the shell of St James. This is because many centuries ago, nobody seems to know quite when or why, the scallop shell became adopted as the symbol of Saint James, and an absolutely essential accessory for any pilgrim journeying to the saint's traditional burial site at Compostela in north-western Spain. By the late 12th century, large scallop shells were definitely being sold to pilgrims at St James' shrine at what became known as Santiago de Compostela, to carry on their way home as a symbol and sort of souvenir of their pilgrimage. Since the only large pectinid mollusc living in the immediate vicinity of Santiago de Compostela is *Pecten maximus*, this was undoubtedly the creature whose shells were sold to the pilgrims, no doubt after the succulent beasts that had produced them had been eaten, probably by the family of the souvenir seller! As we have seen, it was this very species that was known in the Middle Ages as *scelpe*, the word corrupted first by the French in escalope and then by the English into scallop. Hey presto, 'scallop', 'Coquille Saint Jacques' and *Pecten maximus* are all names for the same beast.

21 What are green-lipped mussels?

Green-lipped mussels (*Perna canaliculus*), also known as New Zealand mussels or greenshell mussels, are bivalve molluscs in the same family – the Mytilidae – that also contains the European mussel. As their common names suggest, they are characterised by having a distinct green lip around the otherwise dark brown or greenish shell, and by being originally largely restricted to New Zealand intertidal and shallow waters, though it is now something of a pest in Australian waters.

Partly because it is a good deal larger than its European cousin, growing to a shell length in excess of 20cm (8in), it has been exported in considerable quantities to Europe and North America since the 1970s and 80s. It is now economically extremely important in New Zealand and is intensively farmed, particularly in the Marlborough Sound area in the northern part of South Island. Probably because of its size and relative cheapness despite the transport costs, the green-lipped mussel is now ousting the native European mussel in restaurants and supermarket fish counters. This is a shame because these Kiwi imports are not a patch on our native mussels when it comes to flavour and in my not very humble opinion should be shunned. Quite apart from the taste, it is surely not environmentally sensible to ship mussels, including their inedible and heavy shells, halfway round the world.

European mussels (*Mytilus edulis*) grow only to a length of about 10 or 12cm (4–5in) and take up to 10 years to reach that size. However, they are usually eaten a good deal smaller, at a length of a couple of inches or so, which they reach after about 3 years in decent feeding conditions. Because they feed on tiny planktonic organisms, particularly microscopic plants, filtered from the large volumes of water that they waft through their gills, all mussels are susceptible to accumulating toxins in polluted waters and causing food poisoning when eaten (see also Q4). They are apparently particularly susceptible in the breeding season, which is during the summer in northern European waters. This is why mussels and oysters were traditionally shunned when there is no 'r' in the month[33] – that is, from May to August – and were rather unfashionable for many years when our inshore waters were widely, and justifiably, considered to be pretty dirty. However, the situation has improved considerably in recent years and most European mussels now offered for sale have been cultivated on ropes suspended beneath rafts floating in clean waters – in the UK, mussel cultivation is carried out particularly in sea lochs in Scotland and Ireland. So assuming that you don't have a shellfish allergy you can tuck into European mussels with confidence. Bon appétit!

---

33   Inappropriate, of course, for creatures from the southern hemisphere.

22 What is tomalley?

During the 2 December 2009 edition of the popular BBC quiz show *Eggheads*, the egghead whizz-kid Kevin was asked if the delicacy 'tomalley' comes from lobsters, crabs or clams. Kevin admitted that he had never heard the term and guessed, wrongly, that it comes from clams. It turned out that tomalley (sometimes spelt 'tomale') is a greenish gunge made by mashing up, and possibly cooking, bits of a lobster's innards. Kevin's ignorance debarred him from taking part in the final and the challengers went on to a resounding victory over the eggheads, walking away with £17,000, much to my delight and, I am pretty sure, the delight of lots of viewers.

But since I, like Kevin, had never heard the term 'tomalley' despite a lifetime's involvement with things crustacean, I thought I should find out a bit more about it and share my newfound knowledge with you.

According to the OED, tomalley is possibly a Carib word[34] that refers to the 'liver' of the lobster, more specifically the North American lobster since this is the species that any Caribbean is likely to be familiar with. A lobster's liver, or more properly its digestive gland[35], is a somewhat soft and mushy organ that fills much of the space enclosed by the lobster's main shell or carapace. Most European lobster consumers concentrate on the white meat in the creature's tail and claws, so that the 'offal', including the digestive gland, is usually ignored[36]. Apparently this is a mistake, since the best lobster bisques, stocks and consommés are made using both the tomalley and the female roe or coral, the mature ovaries. Yuk!

Unfortunately for tomalley enthusiasts, eating it comes with a health warning. Among other things, the function of a lobster's digestive gland – like the liver of most beasts that have one – is to deal with any toxins taken in with the food. This means that if the lobster eats anything nasty it is likely to be concentrated in the liver, making this bit particularly toxic to anything that eats it, including humans. For this reason, you have to be a touch careful about eating tomalley to ensure that the lobster from which it comes was not exposed to things like red tides (see Q4). As a result of this danger, the US Food and Drug Administration issued a general warning in July 2008 against eating tomalley derived from lobsters caught off the New England coast. The equivalent Canadian authority was a little less extreme in its May 2008 warning, updated in July 2009, recommending that children should eat no tomalley, while adults should eat no more than the toma-lley from one lobster each day. For most of us, chance would be a fine thing!

---

34 That is, derived from the language of the pre-European inhabitants of the Caribbean islands.
35 Or even more properly the hepatopancreas, since it fulfils the functions of both the liver and the pancreas of many other animals.
36 In contrast, crab eaters routinely consume the crab equivalent to tomalley in the 'brown meat'.

23 What are 'seafood sticks' or 'crab sticks'?

A fairly common item on supermarket fish counters in recent years are curious objects looking a bit like sections of rhubarb stalk, 5–10cm (2–4in) or so long, white through the centre but usually with a pretty violent red or orange outer colour, making them look rather like an old-fashioned stick of seaside rock. They are variously named seafood sticks, crab sticks, fish sticks or even sea legs, crab legs or krab, the latter particularly in the USA.

Despite the names, these products rarely, if ever, contain crabmeat. Instead, they are made up of a fish paste usually referred to in the list of ingredients as 'surimi'. Surimi is a Japanese word meaning 'ground meat' and can refer to more or less any minced-up animal flesh, whether terrestrial or aquatic[37]. In the seafood context the surimi is usually made from the flesh of white fish such as cod or related species like pollack, whiting or hake, but many other species may be used including milkfish, swordfish, various shark species and several intensively farmed freshwater species.

Typically, whatever the origin, the flesh is first separated from the bones and other tissues and then minced, washed and pulverised into a gelatinous paste which is treated with a range of additives, depending on its ultimate intended use. There is nothing particularly wrong with this, but most reports suggest that in its basic form surimi is usually fairly tasteless and, with a water content of about 75%, of limited nutritional value.

The practice of producing surimi seems to date back many hundreds of years in East Asia, but the modern surimi industry was established in Japan in the 1960s to help revitalise the nation's fishing industry and to make use of fish that was otherwise of very limited economic value. Since that time, surimi production has spread to many other countries, principally the USA but also including Thailand, Vietnam, Chile, France, Malaysia and even the Faeroe Islands. Currently, between 2 and 3 million tonnes of fish are used annually for surimi production.

In Asian cultures surimi is often eaten as a food in its own right, though in Japan it is used in fish cakes and fish sausages. In other parts of the world, however,

---

37 This may sound pretty unappetising, but should not be confused with the really nasty stuff usually referred to as MSM (mechanically separated meat) or MRM (mechanically recovered meat), which got a justifiably bad name during the 1980s and '90s. MSM and MRM is a paste produced by forcing pork, beef, turkey or chicken bones and scraps of attached meat through some sort of sieve under high pressure. The technique was used from the 1950s onwards to extract the very last scrap of vaguely edible material from animal carcasses. The resulting rubbish, containing all sorts of unmentionable bits, was, and unfortunately from time to time still is, put into cheap prepared foods like pies, sausages and burgers, and was particularly targeted during the BSE scares.

it is usually used as a constituent of various processed food, such as seafood sticks and crab sticks, because it enables the manufacturer to imitate the texture and taste of more expensive raw materials such as lobster and crab[38].

24 When is a pollack not a pollack?

The pollack or pollock (both pronounced 'pollock', sometimes with unfortunate consequences, as you will see later) is a marine fish species placed by scientists in the same family, the Gadidae, that contains a further 20-odd species including the cods, whitings and haddocks. Gadids are found all over the world, mainly in relatively shallow waters over the continental shelves, but with some species extending into deeper water over the continental slopes. Each of these groups is placed in different genera, each containing a number of distinct species (see Q2); for example, the cods are in the genus *Gadus,* the whitings in *Merlangus,* the haddocks in *Melanogrammus* – and the pollack in *Pollachius.* All of them live on or close to the bottom and feed on more or less anything they can catch, but particularly worms, molluscs, crustaceans and other fish. In turn, they are eaten by seals, dolphins and whales – and especially by humans, because many species are targeted in important fisheries.

In April 2009 pollack hit the headlines in Britain briefly when the supermarket chain Sainsbury's announced that in future they would refer to pollack in their stores as 'colin'. This name change was designed to increase sales of pollack as against other gadoid fishes such as cod and haddock, by encouraging prospective customers who were, according to Sainsbury's spokespersons, embarrassed to use the word pollack! Unsurprisingly, the proposal to name a fish 'colin' prompted a good deal of hilarity. After all, why not name others Fred or Bob? Then it transpired that colin should not be pronounced like the English boy's name but more like 'Kola' because 'colin' is a French name for a cod-like fish – but not mainly, or even necessarily, for what we call the pollack (if we are not too embarrassed). Despite the (justified) claim that the French are much more discerning than the rest of us in their approach to seafood, and possibly to food generally, there seems to be just as much potential for confusion in French when it comes to distinguishing between reasonably similar species as in any other language. The term *colin* in France is used not for the cod, but for the hake, which is more commonly referred to as *merlu* – not to be confused with *merluche,* which refers to dried cod, whereas the French for 'wet' cod is *morue* or sometimes *cabillaud.* Wet haddock is called *églefin,* while dried haddock is called by the French, would you believe, *haddock* – pronounced 'addock!

38   For more details see J.W. Park [Ed] *Surimi and surimi seafood,* Second edition, 2005.

The hakes are also relatives of the cod, in this case in the genus *Merluccius*. But because the hakes have slightly different skeletal characteristics than the other gadids they are sometimes considered to be in a separate family, the Merluccidae. Confusing, isn't it?

PS. The fuss over the pollack's (or pollock's) name seems to have faded away. By November 2009 my local Sainsbury's was consistently *not* using colin but somewhat inconsistently using both pollack and pollock.

25 What are monkfish?

Monkfish (or *lotte* in French) is a name given to rather grotesque-looking fish belonging to the genus *Lophius* in the family Lophiidae, which also contains a number of other genera.

All lophiids are anglerfish, with flattened bodies and huge heads and mouths. They spend most of their time lying stationary, at depths of a few hundred metres, on the sandy or muddy sea floor, against which their rough and warty skin is perfectly camouflaged. The upper jaw carries a strange structure evolved from modified fin rays, which is used like an animated fishing rod, dangled over the angler's mouth to attract potential prey, particularly other fish. Once a potential food morsel wanders within striking distance the angler suddenly opens its mouth and engulfs the hapless prey.

Figure 18
Monkfish offered for sale in the fish market at Ceuta, the Spanish enclave in Morocco. Presumably because the fish is so unattractive in its normal orientation, it is displayed here upside down showing its rather more appealing white and smooth underside, with its small pectoral fins looking a bit like eyebrows.

The origin of the name monk or monkfish is a bit unclear, but the same name is used for a group of bottom-living shark-like fish belonging to the genus *Squatina*, totally unrelated to *Lophius*, but with a broadly similar body shape. So it is possible that the name refers to the vague resemblance of both groups of fishes to a monk's cowl.

Because of their rather offputting appearance, monkfish are called by a number of other unflattering names such as headfish, fishing-frog, frogfish or even sea-devil. But their ugliness belies their culinary value, for their flesh is of a consistency and taste that makes them highly sought after – and therefore very expensive!

26 What are basa fish?

A relatively recent, but increasingly common, addition to European and North American fish counters is something called basa and almost always presented as fillets rather than the whole fish. The basa fish, *Pangasius bocourti*, is a type of catfish native to the Mekong Delta in Vietnam and the Chao Phraya basin in Thailand. It belongs to the family Pangasidae, sometimes called shark catfish because of their vaguely shark-like shape, and particularly because several species have large triangular dorsal fins, again vaguely reminiscent of sharks. In fact, they are true bony fish like salmon, herring, cod and so on, and are not at all closely related to the sharks with their non-bony cartilaginous skeletons.

The Pangasidae contains about 30 species of mainly herbivorous fish found in fresh and brackish waters in southern Asia. Basa is by far the most important, commercially, with large quantities being exported to North America and Europe. In the USA the fish is usually sold under the names basa or bocourti, the use of the term 'catfish' being outlawed by the US Food and Drug Administration to protect the American domestic catfish-rearing industry which is based on so-called 'true' catfish of the family Ictaluridae. In the UK and continental Europe it is also sold as basa fish, but may be marketed as river cobbler, Vietnamese river cobbler[39] or panga.

Basa flesh is firm and white, with a consistency not unlike cod and pollack. With a retail price about half that of cod, it is often offered as a cheaper alternative and is sometimes even fraudulently sold as cod by unscrupulous fish-and-chip-shopkeepers.

---

39   I have certainly seen it labelled 'river cobbler' in my local Sainsbury's in Alton in Hampshire.

Figure 19
Fresh European sea bass landed in Portsmouth and offered for sale the same day at a farmers' market in Alton, Hampshire.

27 What are sea bass?

The European sea bass, *Dicentrarchus labrax* (Fig 19), is a medium to large shallow water (to about 100m/330ft) fish, with a fairly sharp 'nose', silvery sides and two prominent dorsal fins. It is found from Norway and possibly Iceland in the north to Senegal in the south and is also present in the Mediterranean and Black Seas. It has long been highly prized as a food fish in southern Europe, where it is known under several different names including lubina or róbalo in Spain, bronzini or branzini in Italy and lavraki in Greece.

Throughout its range it spends considerable time in inshore waters and may even enter estuaries. Since it can grow to a length of more than a metre (3ft) and may weigh 15kg (33lb), it is a popular game fish. Until relatively recently it was known in the UK simply as bass since it is the only representative of its family, the Moronidea, in British seawaters. The addition of the unnecessary 'sea' to its name seems to have come about as a result of its popularity with celebrity chefs, possibly to distinguish it from the many, rather less appreciated freshwater 'basses'.

28 What are sea bream?

Sea bream are small- to medium-sized deep-bodied fish, somewhat flattened from side to side and usually with quite silvery scales. There are several species world-wide, most belonging to the family Sparidae.

In the north-east Atlantic there are two main sparids, the red or blackspot sea bream[40], *Pagellus bogaraveo,* so-called because of its reddish fins and the prominent black spot above and behind the eye, and the black sea bream[41], *Spondyliosoma cantharus,* which is much darker than the red sea bream and has no prominent spot.

The red sea bream reaches a length of 70cm (27in) but is usually caught and sold at a length of about 30cm (12in). It lives mostly in mid-water at depths between about 150 and 300m (500–1,000ft) and is found from off the coast of Norway in the north to the Canary Islands and Mauritania in the south. It also extends into the western Mediterranean as far east as Sicily. Red sea bream feed mainly on crustaceans, molluscs, worms and small fish, both in mid-water and on the muddy sea floor.

The black sea bream has a rather similar geographical distribution to the red sea bream but extends somewhat further south, to northern Namibia, and also reaches the Black Sea. It is usually found in somewhat shallower water over sandy bottoms and on seagrass beds, but feeds on broadly the same types of food.

Both species change sex during their life histories, the red sea bream starting off life as males and changing into females at a length of some 20–30cm (8–12in), while the black sea bream does much the same, but starts off as female and later becomes male.

29 What is the orange roughy?

The orange roughy is a deep-water fish, which lives close to the bottom at depths ranging from about 200 to 2,000m (650–6,560ft). It is a deep-bodied and fairly large fish, growing to a length of about 75cm (30in) and weighing up to 7kg (15lb). In life its skin is a rather deep red colour, becoming more orange after death. Its scientific name is *Hoplostethus atlanticus,* from which you might guess that it lives in the Atlantic Ocean – and you would be right, because it was first

---

40   Also known as dorade rose in France and besugo in Spain.
41   Known as dorade grise in France, chopa in Spain and, somewhat non-pc, as the 'old wife' in the Isle of Man!

described in 1889 from a specimen collected near the Azores and is now known from lots of places around the North Atlantic. But it is also found in various other parts of the world, including Australian and New Zealand waters. Until 30 or so years ago the orange roughy was familiar only to deep-sea biologists and had no common name other than the pretty unflattering title 'slimehead', which is applied to the family in which fish specialists place it. Then, in the late 1970s, seemingly vast populations were found over deep submarine banks around New Zealand and its outlying islands and a fishery rapidly developed. The appellation 'slimehead' was clearly not going to attract many customers, so fish marketers in NZ coined the new name to promote the fish, especially in the United States. A major US market quickly became established – and still exists – encouraging orange roughy fisheries to start up in various parts of the Indo-Pacific region. From a standing start the annual catch of orange roughy rocketed to 54,000 tonnes in 1988/89, but then equally rapidly declined, until by 1997/98 only 16,000 tonnes were caught. It is still being caught – and eaten – in considerable quantities, but it is now on Australia's list of endangered species and the NGO (Non-Governmental Organisation) Sea Watch advises health- and sustainability-minded Americans to avoid it. So what went wrong?

Basically, it was because the fishing industry targeted the species without knowing the first thing about its biology, a fatal error for any attempt to exploit a wild population. It turns out that the orange roughy, like many other deep-water species, is long-lived and slow-growing. In fact, some estimates suggest that they live for up to 150 years! These figures have been challenged, particularly by the fishing industry, even though they are based on analyses of radioisotopes and growth rings in the ear bones or otoliths, techniques that have a long and trusted history in age determination in shallow-water species. But even if they don't live quite this long, scientists are agreed that orange roughy live a long, long time. More importantly, though, they also agree that they do not reach sexual maturity until they are at least 30 years old. This means that the populations are extremely vulnerable to overfishing because many of the fish caught have never reached an age when they could breed – a recipe for disaster.

Despite the New Zealand authorities implementing more and more stringent quotas, the catch rates are continuing to fall, a clear indication of overfishing. But there is an even more worrying and somewhat puzzling twist to the orange roughy story. It appears that the numbers of orange roughy in New Zealand populations has fallen dramatically but without any substantial change in the size distribution of the animals caught. This is very strange, because in normal over-fishing situations, the biggest (and oldest) animals are targeted first so that the average size of fish caught decreases with time. A possible explanation is that orange roughy populations, and possibly those of many other deep-sea species, are characterised by what is called a 'steady state', in which there is a very slow through-put of energy resulting in slow growth rates and low levels of recruitment. This situation is a bit like that in a very mature forest. And just as a forest is dominated by lots of big trees, with ages ranging from a few decades to hundreds of years, orange roughy populations may also be composed of lots of big, but not necessarily very old animals, and rather few very little ones. If you chop down lots of big forest trees all at the same time it will take a long time to replace them, and if you chop too many down, the forest may never recover.

In exactly the same way, it seems that the antipodean roughy populations could support a trawl fishery only at much lower levels than those to which they have been subjected, hence the collapse. Unfortunately, the market for orange roughy, particularly in the USA, is still buoyant, encouraging suppliers to search for new populations to exploit. The search has now extended to the north-eastern Atlantic, back to its 'original' home. Although some fishable populations have been found and there has been a small but consistent French orange roughy fishery from waters off north-western Europe since the early 1990s, so far it seems that no large North Atlantic concentrations comparable with the New Zealand ones have been found. If they ever are, let's hope that any exploitation is kept at a level that the species can withstand. But don't hold your breath. Fishermen as a group are not renowned as the fastest learners!

30 What are butterfish?

Butterfish is appearing increasingly on gastro-pub menus. So what is it? Well, it is most likely to have been imported either from the eastern seaboard of the United States or from the western Pacific.

The American version is, not surprisingly, more properly referred to as the American butterfish, *Peprilus triacanthus*[42]. It belongs to the family Stromateidae, which contains a total of about 17 species living in shallow waters of the Atlantic and the Indo-Pacific region, all more or less deep-bodied fish, fairly circular in side view and flattened from side to side.

The American butterfish is found off the Atlantic coast of North America from around Newfoundland in the north to Florida in the south, but most abundantly in the central parts of this range. It is a relatively small fish, generally growing to

---

42   The butterfish is apparently also known as dollarfish (presumably on account of its shape), shiner, skipjack, sheepshead or harvestfish, though this last name is usually restricted to its close relative *Peprilus alepidotus*.

no more than about 22cm (9in) long and weighing up to about 500g (1lb). Butter-fish are primarily mid-water fish feeding on small fish, squid and crustaceans. They reach sexual maturity at about two years of age and probably rarely live longer than 3 or 4 years.

American butterfish have been fished commercially for many years but catches reached a peak at about 34,000 metric tonnes in the mid 1970s, since when land-ings have generally decreased, reaching a reported record low of only 430 metric tonnes in 2005.

Such low catches are certainly not sufficient to satisfy international demand, so butterfish on the menu in the last few years may instead refer to the Japanese butterfish, *Psenopsis anomula*[43]. Although superficially quite similar to the Amer-ican butterfish, the Japanese butterfish belongs to a quite different family, the Centrolophidae, also known collectively as medusafish because of their habit of associating with jellyfish, apparently to provide some protection from predators. It is found in shallow waters of the western North Pacific, where it is a popular food fish and is extensively exploited by Japanese and Taiwanese fishermen.

These species are not to be confused with the European butterfish or gunnel, *Pholis* (or *Centronotus*) *gunnellus*. Although this butterfish grows to about 25cm (10in) long, it is a very slim, rather eel-shaped, little fish and is emphatically not commercially exploited. It is common off the coasts of north-western Europe, including between the tidemarks on rocky shores, and is one of the most common fishes found by children searching in rock pools and under seaweeds at low tide. It is notoriously difficult to pick up with the fingers – hence its common name.

31 What are swordfish?

The swordfish is a large, fast-swimming, predatory fish characterised by a long, sword-like extension of the upper jaw – hence both its common name and its scientific name, *Xiphias gladius, gladius* being the Latin word for 'sword'.

Scientists place the swordfish in the family Xiphiidae, of which it is the sole living representative. But an alternative name is 'broadbill', because the swordfish is grouped with the billfishes, also large predatory fish, which belong to a separate family, the Istiophoridae, and include the sailfish and marlin.

All billfishes have sword-like bills, but none as long as the true swordfish.

Billfishes, including the swordfish, are widely distributed in the warmer parts

43   Also known as ibodai in Japan and, somewhat inexplicably, as the melon seed or by the even more unappealing name of wart perch.

of the Pacific, Indian and Atlantic Oceans and in the Mediterranean. They are popular targets of sport fishermen both because of their size (up to more than 4m/13ft long and weighing 600kg/1,320lb or more) and because of their power and agility.

Swordfish flesh is oily, firm and usually somewhat dark in colour, rather like tuna. Because of the size, swordfish can be presented as steaks very suitable for grilling and it is therefore a popular eating fish. Until relatively recently, swordfish were harvested for human consumption in fairly small numbers. But with the huge expansion in longline fishing over the last 20 years or so, swordfish catches have increased enormously, often claimed to be an accidental 'bycatch' by fishermen said to be fishing for quite different species, such as tuna. The effect, nevertheless, is that while the survival of swordfish as a species is not considered to be seriously in danger, the populations in many areas of the oceans have become seriously depleted.

32 What are black halibut?

All halibut are flatfish belonging to the same family, the Pleuronectidae that contains the plaice, flounder and lemon sole[44]. They all begin life as symmetrical larvae swimming in mid-water and with one eye on either side of the body. As they develop, however, the left eye begins to migrate upwards over the top of the head to join its opposite number on the right-hand side. When the process is complete, at a length of 2–3cm (1in), the fish – by now rather flattened – settles down on the bottom, lying on its left side so that the eyes are now on the upper surface of the body[45].

True or white halibut belong to the genus *Hippoglossus,* with one major species in the North Atlantic (*H. hippoglossus)* and one in the North Pacific (*H. stenolepis),* both living mainly close to the bottom in depths down to several hundreds of metres. The Atlantic halibut is the largest flatfish in the oceans, growing to lengths well in excess of 2m (7ft) and weighing more than 300kg (660lb), while the Pacific halibut is a little smaller, though still attaining weights of more than 200kg (440lb). Both species have firm, highly prized flesh, and have been the subject of important commercial fisheries for well over a century in the Pacific and for several hundreds of years in the Atlantic. However, the Atlantic halibut popula-tions have been severely overfished in recent decades so that it is now in short

---

44   But not the turbot, brill or true sole or Dover sole.
45   Although the vast majority of pleuronectids lie on their left sides, occasional individuals lie on their right sides. In just the same way, most turbot lie on their right sides, but odd ones lie down the other way.

supply and the black halibut is often offered as a cheaper and more readily obtained alternative.

Unfortunately, the black halibut (*Reinhardtius hippoglossoides*), also known as Greenland or mock halibut, is a much inferior fish for eating, with much softer, rather watery, flesh.

33 What is hoki?

Hoki (Latin name *Macruronus novaezelundiae*) – also known as New Zealand whiting, blue grenadier, whiptail or whiptail hake – is a slender-bodied, relatively deep-water marine fish widely distributed in the south-western Pacific, particularly around New Zealand and southern Australia. It grows to a length of a metre (3ft) or so, lives mostly on or close to the sea floor at depths down to about 1,000m (3,280ft) and feeds mainly on small fish, crustaceans and squid. Although it is placed in the same family, the Merlucciidae, that contains the hakes and other cod relatives, it has a long and slender tail quite unlike most hakes.

The New Zealand hoki fishery, using bottom or mid-water trawls, is a relatively young one, but the annual catch rapidly expanded to about 100,000 tonnes in the late 1990s, mostly exported to the USA, Europe, Japan and Australia. In 2001 the Marine Stewardship Council (MSC) (see Q51) certified it as a well-managed and sustainable fishery and recertified it in 2007. However, since that time the catches have oscillated rather wildly, and in 2010 Greenpeace International added hoki to its red list. Partly as a result, the appropriateness of the MSC certification of a number of other fisheries has been questioned by conservationists.

34 What is coley?

The coley, more properly called the coalfish or saithe in Scotland, is a relative of the cod which has had something of a roller-coaster ride in popularity over the last 50 or so years. After a long period of rather moderate demand it experienced a surge in popularity in British fish and chip shops when cod supplies fell dramatically during the cod wars of the 1960s and 1970s. Then it went out of favour again until the effects of overfishing of cod and haddock made it an attractive alternative. It is now widely available in supermarkets and fishmongers, and usually sells for about half the price of cod.

As its Latin name, *Pollachius virens*, suggests, it is rather more closely related to the pollack than to the cod, but is easily distinguished from the pollack in outward appearance by its very dark, almost black back compared with the greenish-yellow of the pollack and its slightly forked tail fin.

Once filleted the coalfish is even more distinct because its flesh has a rather blue or grey colour in contrast to the much whiter flesh of pollack, haddock and cod. This clearly makes it less attractive to modern consumers and has almost certainly contributed to its relative unpopularity in the past. This is a shame because it makes extremely good eating and in most areas of the north Atlantic its populations are much less overfished than those of other cod-like species.

Hugh Fearnley-Whittingstall and Nick Fisher (in *The River Cottage Fish Book*, Bloomsbury Publishing) say that in the nineteenth century coley was very important in the British diet and was known as more than fifty different regional names. I am sure they are right, but I think that it has always been considered to be a slightly inferior alternative to cod and pollack partly because of its appearance and the associated mythology. I remember that when I was a student on the Isle of Man in the early 1960s, alongside its Manx name of blockan, the poor old coley was also given a much less attractive appellation indicating that it was believed, quite unjustifiably, to congregate around sewage outlets!

III

Ocean Facts and Figures

Do Whales...? included quite a big section on ocean facts and figures covering most of the basic stuff like how big and deep the oceans are, where all the water came from and what defines the various bits into which we somewhat arbitrarily divide them, like Continental Shelves, Continental Slopes, Abyssal Plains and so on. It would have been inappropriate to repeat this sort of material here. Instead, I've tried to answer some more rather general questions about things like manganese nodules, oil and gas, methane clathrates and so on, but also a few more specific topics ranging from very local ones like the width of the Strait of Gibraltar to somewhat broader ones like the Bermuda Triangle, the Sargasso Sea and the SOFAR channel.

35 Is there a maximum depth that things will sink to in the ocean?

Basically, no, but please read on.

In the 19th century, and in some quarters much more recently, it was widely believed that as the pressure increases with increasing depth in the ocean[46], the water itself is squeezed so that it becomes more and more dense. Eventually, at the bottom of the deepest oceans the water would be as dense or heavy as liquid lead or gold! As a result, anything sinking from the surface would eventually reach

---

46   *Do Whales...?* explained how pressure increases with depth in the sea by approximately one atmosphere (that is 1kg per square cm or 15lb per square inch) for every 10m (33ft). So at a depth of 1,000m (3,280ft) the pressure is about 100 atmospheres, that is about 100kg per square cm or 1,500lb per square inch. At the bottom of the deepest part of the ocean, where the depth is about 11km (7 miles), the pressure is a bone-crunching more than a metric tonne per square cm or 16,500lb/7.5 tons per square inch.

a point where its weight would be equal to the same volume of water. At this point it would stop sinking and simply float suspended in the water column. Different materials would sink to different levels, of course, producing a sort of layer cake in the ocean with lighter materials floating at shallower depths and only the very heaviest things, such as cannon balls and gold bars, sinking to the very bottom of the ocean. A particularly ghoulish aspect of this idea was the belief that at some unspecified level in the sea the remains of drowned sailors would float perpetually until they eventually disintegrated or were eaten!

For all practical purposes this is nonsense. Seawater is very slightly compressible and, as a result, does become a little heavier with depth in the ocean. But the effect is so small that more or less anything that will sink through the top metre or two will, given time, eventually reach the sea floor, whatever the depth. However, the density of seawater is affected by its saltiness and particularly by its temperature much more than by the pressure. Although this is extremely important in separating the deep currents of the oceans, the effect is generally far too small to affect most things sinking in the sea. But there are some strange places where this is not true. In a few remarkable parts of the sea floor, notably in the Gulf of Mexico, in the Mediterranean and in the Red Sea, concentrated brines seep out of the sea floor and accumulate as lakes of extremely salt water in depressions in the seabed. These lakes are extremely toxic to most marine organisms and are inhabited only by some special-ised bacteria. But the brine filling the lakes can be so dense that it can act as a barrier through which at least some objects, including submersibles, won't sink!

I was careful to write at the beginning of that last paragraph that '... more or less anything ...' that will sink at the surface will eventually reach the bottom. The fact that I couldn't truthfully write 'anything' here has been very important for our understanding of the deep currents in the oceans, thanks to a very clever British physical oceanographer, Dr John Swallow, who was studying the deep circulation in the 1950s. John Swallow realised that, though seawater is not very compressible, it is much more so than many solids, including metals. So, thought John, it should be possible to make an incompressible float that could be weighted so that it would just sink at the surface but, because of the compressibility of the water, would become neutrally buoyant at some predetermined depth where it would stop sinking and would drift horizontally with the current. If you could place such floats at different depths and at different places in the deep ocean and then track them as they drifted along, the results would be invaluable in understanding how the oceans work. After a lot of calculations and considerable lateral thinking, John came to the conclusion that standard aluminium scaffold poles would, with a bit of clever jigging, make ideal floats, capable of carrying little battery-operated 'pingers' emitting a sound signal so that their movements could be tracked from the surface. And it worked!

From early experiments in a laboratory in deepest Surrey in southern England, these ideas developed into an international programme in which hundreds of 'Swallow floats' were, and still are, deployed into the oceans of the world and their movements monitored by surface ships. The buoyancy of each float is carefully measured and then adjusted with the addition of tiny weights calculated to carry it to a specific depth before it becomes neutrally buoyant and begins its horizontal journey, periodically 'pinging' to tell its monitoring ship exactly where it is.

Eventually, of course, the batteries die and the floats stop sending out their sound signals. But many of them presumably continue to float gently along in the inky blackness of the deep sea, just as the old mariners imagined corpses and cannon balls did! So although the old guys were quite wrong, there was just enough of a germ of truth in their crazy ideas to enable oceanographers to unravel the mysteries of the deep ocean circulation.

36 Did the Mediterranean really dry up once?

Yes, about 6 million years ago; and in the unlikely event that the Strait of Gibraltar became blocked up, the Mediterranean would dry out again in a matter of a thousand years or so.

The reason is that the Mediterranean is a strange and interesting sea, with a very curious water budget – that is, the balance between the incoming and outgoing water. The sea was formed about 20 million years ago when the African tectonic plate collided with the Eurasian plate, enclosing a great expanse of sea between them. First, the eastern end closed up when present-day Arabia collided with what became Turkey and Iran, leaving the Persian Gulf between them. What is now the Red Sea was already in existence between Arabia and north-eastern Africa, but there was no connection with the eastern Mediterranean[47]. Some time later, the western end closed and the drying out process began because the water balance situation then was, if anything, even more extreme than it is today.

The modern Mediterranean has a total surface area of about 2.5 million km^2 (1 million square miles) and a mean depth of about 1,500m (5,000ft). This gives it a volume of about 3.75 million km^3 (900,000 cubic miles). The annual water loss by evaporation from its surface is about 4,700 km^3 (1,130 cubic miles). About 1,200 km^3 (300 cubic miles) falls back as rain each year, but the Mediterranean has few major rivers apart from the Rhone, the Nile and, via the Black Sea, the Danube. Consequently, the total annual supply from all river sources is only about 250 km^3 (60 cubic miles), leaving a net annual deficit of some 3,250 km^3 (770 cubic miles).

47 A situation that persisted until 1869, when the Suez Canal was opened.

This deficit is nowadays made up by Atlantic water entering the Mediterranean in the form of a strong and almost continuous eastward-flowing surface current through the Strait of Gibraltar. In fact this input is so large that there is a smaller, but very significant, outward flow of Mediterranean water beneath the surface current.

Six million years ago, however, the Strait of Gibraltar didn't exist, so there was no way for the Mediterranean's annual water deficit to be replaced by Atlantic water. Within a geological blink of an eye, possibly a few hundred years, the sea dried out almost completely, leaving just a few very salt lakes in its deepest parts. We know this because deep beneath the bed of the present Mediterranean there are huge deposits of salt, in places almost 2km (1¼ miles) thick, left there as the sea dried out all those aeons ago. In fact, there is so much salt that it seems it could not have been produced by the evaporation of just a single Mediterranean-full, so to speak. So it appears that during the 700,000 years or so that the dry Mediterranean existed there were periodic 'spills' of water over the sill between modern Morocco and Spain, adding to the salt layers as they, in turn, evaporated.

The bottom of this gigantic hot and arid depression must have been a pretty inhospitable environment, not least because the removal of the huge weight of water will have caused major movements of the earth's crust and lots of volcanic activity. Eventually, about 5.3 million years ago, the narrow junction with the open Atlantic, today only 14km (9 miles) wide at its narrowest point, opened for the last time and the previous intermittent spills of water were replaced by a vast cataract that filled the Mediterranean basin in about 60 years. It must have been an awesome sight, though there were, of course, no humans on earth to witness it. Geologists estimate that the stupendous waterfall was as much as 3,000m (10,000ft) high (that is, 50 times as high as the Niagara Falls), while water poured over it at a rate of about 170 cubic km (40 cubic miles) a day, equivalent to about a thousand Niagaras!

And it has been full ever since.

37 How narrow (or wide) is the Strait of Gibraltar?

The Strait (not Straits, because there is only one) of Gibraltar is the narrow channel between Spain in the north and Morocco in the south, linking the Mediterranean Sea with the Atlantic Ocean. At its narrowest point the Strait is only 7.7 nautical miles or 14.25km (9 miles) wide, while its depth ranges from 300 to 900m (about 1,000–3,000ft).

It is named for the famous rock of Gibraltar, which, in turn, gets its name from the Arabic *Jebel al-Tariq*, meaning 'Tariq's mountain'. The Tariq in question was the Berber chief who supposedly first landed on the rock in 711AD and at the very beginning of the Muslim occupation of southern Spain, which was to last until 1492[48]. The rock itself forms a narrow limestone promontory jutting out into the Strait from mainland Spain, with a maximum height of 426m (1,398ft). It has been an overseas territory of Great Britain since the Treaty of Utrecht in 1713, following the War of the Spanish Succession. This British possession understandably continues to be a contentious issue for Spain, not least because of its strategic importance at the mouth of the Mediterranean.

To the ancient Greeks, the Strait marked the western limit of the known world, flanked by two mountains, which became known as the Pillars of Hercules. While the rock of Gibraltar is undoubtedly the northern of the two pillars, the identity of the southern (African) one is disputed. The two main contenders are Jebel Musa in Morocco, standing 851m (2,790ft) high, or the much lower (204m/669ft high) Monte Hacho in Ceuta, the tiny (28 km²) Spanish enclave on the North African side of the Strait (see Fig 20). Just as the Spanish claim ownership of Gibraltar, the Moroccans think Ceuta should be part of Morocco!

Figure 20
The statue of Hercules and his pillars dominating the approach to the harbour in Ceuta. Whether you see him as pulling the two pillars together or forcing them apart depends on which version of Hercules' tenth labour you choose. According to one version, Hercules smashed his way out of the Mediterranean, thus opening the Strait of Gibraltar. The other version has him closing the gap to prevent Atlantic monsters from entering the Mediterranean.

48   See John Julius Norwich's excellent *The Middle Sea: A History of the Mediterranean*, published by Chatto & Windus in 2006.

38 Why is the Black Sea called the Black Sea?

Not, apparently, because of its colour. But I didn't know that when my wife and I first set eyes on the sea from the deck of a cruise ship in October 2008. We were among the thousands of cruise-ship passengers who visit the Black Sea each year in the post-Soviet Union era. So when several of my fellow passengers asked me where the name comes from, I admitted that I didn't know – but I hazarded a guess.

I knew that the Black Sea is a quite special place with some very peculiar characteristics. First, it is a land-locked sea, roughly 1,000km (620 miles) from west to east and 500km (310 miles) from north to south, bordered by Turkey to the south, Bulgaria and Romania to the west, Ukraine to the north and Russia and Georgia to the east. With a surface area of just under half a million square kilometres (193,000 square miles), and a maximum depth of 2,200m (7,200ft), it is only about one fifth the area of the Mediterranean. It receives a significant inflow of river water, particularly from the Danube, the Dnieper and the Don, and has a net outflow of about 250km^3 (60 cubic miles) of water each year to the Mediterranean through the Bosphorus, the Sea of Marmara and the Dardanelles. This warm Black Sea surface water is only about half as salty as the true Mediterranean water and, just like at the Strait of Gibraltar (see Q37), there is a flow of warmer, but saltier and heavier, Mediterranean water into the Black Sea beneath the outflowing surface water. This results in a huge pool of heavy, relatively salt water in the deeper parts of the sea, overlaid by a surface layer of lighter, less saline water between about 100 and 200m (330–660ft) thick. Because of the major density difference between the two layers they are essentially isolated from one another, with very important consequences.

The surface layers are normally well oxygenated and supplied with ample nutrients carried down by the rivers. As a result, the Black Sea in historic times has been very productive and, as recently as the 1980s, total annual fish catches reached more than 500,000 tonnes. Quite naturally, and for thousands if not millions of years, lots of organic matter in the form of dead and dying remains of planktonic and larger organisms, as well as their faecal material, has sunk from the surface layer into the deeper, more or less stagnant bottom water. As this material is broken down by bacteria, any remains of oxygen brought in from the Mediterranean is quickly used up and the vast bulk of the deeper parts of the Black Sea are therefore anoxic (totally devoid of oxygen). The breakdown of organic matter in the absence of oxygen results in the production of hydrogen sulphide, the 'bad egg' gas, and thick, black, foul-smelling bottom sediments wherever the depth is more than about 200m (660ft). Since local fishermen would have been familiar with this mucky stuff for hundreds of years, I assumed that the name came from that. But I was wrong.

Nobody seems to know for certain, but there are two main theories about where the name came from. One is based on the idea that the ancients found the Black Sea a very inhospitable place, subject to lots of bad, and therefore dull or dark, weather – hence the black epithet. This seems to me to be pretty unconvincing, not least because there isn't much evidence to suggest that the Black Sea is more prone to bad weather than the nearby bits of the Mediterranean. So I am much more attracted to the second, slightly whimsical, explanation. This suggests that it got its name from the Ottoman Turks, who called it the *Karadeniz,* the 'Kara' part meaning 'black'. The modern names in all the languages of the surrounding countries, like the English version, seem to have been derived from the Turkish and therefore also mean 'Black Sea'. But the little twist in this explanation is that the medieval Turks were almost certainly not using *kara* in its literal sense, but rather in a slightly metaphorical sense. At the time, the cardinal points of the compass – north, south, east and west – were represented by colours, with north being represented by black. What better way to name the Turk's northern sea than to label it with the colour representing that direction? So in medieval Turkish the name *Karadeniz* probably signified 'North Sea[49]' as much as it did 'Black Sea'.

In the same way, the Turkish word *kizil* means red, and red denoted the south. Surprise, surprise, the Red Sea, to the south of the Turkish Empire, was called *Kizil Deniz* again apparently without any reference to its colour.

39 What is the Black Sea deluge theory?

The story of Noah's Ark and the associated flood is one of the most iconic traditions in all countries associated with the so-called Abrahamic religions – that is, Judaism, Christianity and Islam – that originated roughly in what we now call the Middle East. A similar flood tradition exists in other monotheistic faiths from the same region, but not in the major non-Abrahamic religions originating in India and eastern Asia. This difference has intrigued many commentators over the years and led some to believe that the story might be based on a real event somewhere in the Middle Eastern area.

The basic story is that the 600-year-old righteous man, Noah, was commanded by God to build a vessel (the ark) in which to save his own family and the world's

---

49   The name North Sea for the more familiar one between the UK and northern Europe goes back to the Romans, who called it *Oceanus Septentrionalis*, that is, northern ocean (the septentrionalis bit apparently referring to the seven stars in the Great Bear constellation near the North Pole). However, for a long period during the Middle Ages, right up to the end of the 18th century, it was more usually known as the *Mare Germanicum* or German Sea. This seems to me to be an eminently more appropriate name for the Brits and Scandinavians, for whom the North Sea is hardly in the north, but it is unlikely to change!

animals from a worldwide flood, to be sent by the Lord to destroy most of the earth because of man's wickedness. Once Noah's family and the animals[50] were safely in the ark, God sent the rains, which persisted for 40 days and 40 nights until all the mountains of the earth were covered. Eventually the rains, stopped and the waters began to recede. In the seventh month after the start of the rains, the ark came to rest on Mount Ararat, the exact position of which is still disputed, but is generally agreed to be somewhere in present-day Iran or Turkey. Three months later, according to Genesis, the tops of various mountains emerged from the water and Noah sent out the raven and the dove to see how much dry land there was. Then, a couple of months later, on the first day of the first month of Noah's 601st year, he took the cover off the ark and saw that things were drying out nicely. Finally, on the 27th of the second month the earth was back to normal, Noah's family and the animals left the ark and the rest is history.

For many centuries the Abrahamic religions accepted the flood story more or less literally, though in Islam there is apparently no specific reference to a world-wide flood. However, by the 18th century the advance of scientific knowledge caused many aspects of the story to be questioned, including the idea that any flood could have been universal, not least because there is simply not enough water on earth to go round. But this has not stopped flood enthusiasts searching for evidence in support of the story, ranging from biblical literalists looking for remains of the ark itself, to more cynical commentators seeking signs of geological evidence. The 'deluge theory', put forward by geologists William Ryan and Walter Pitman in 1997[51], sits firmly in this second category.

Basically, the theory suggests that about 7,500 years ago the Black Sea and the Mediterranean were separated and, at the time, the Black Sea occupied a much smaller area than it does now. This was because after the end of the last ice age, around 10,000 years ago, the retreat of the glaciers affected the rivers that had previously fed into the Black Sea and the Caspian, which, in turn, had emptied into what we now call the Aegean. The flow of some of the rivers was reduced, while others were diverted from their original courses and no longer flowed into the Black and Caspian Seas. As a result, the areas of both the Black Sea and the Caspian were significantly reduced by evaporation, the connection between the Black Sea and the Mediterranean disappeared, and the Black Sea was reduced to

---

50   Two by two, you remember, and with seven such pairs of each of the designated 'clean' animals, but only one pair of the 'unclean' ones.
51   Ryan and Pitman published their theory in the very respectable academic journal *Marine Geology* in 1997 under the title 'An abrupt drowning of the Black Sea shelf'. But the juicy bits hit the public headlines in *The New York Times* in December 1996. Lots of relevant, and some irrelevant stuff is available on the internet. Start with Wikipedia, which I have used extensively, and then move on, but with a good deal of cynicism!

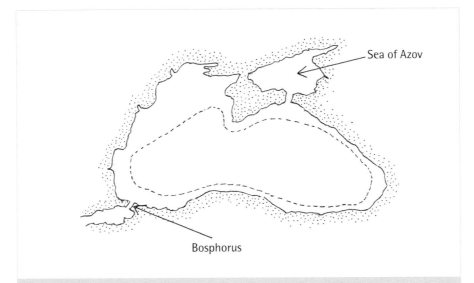

Figure 21
The area occupied by the Black Sea immediately before the 'deluge' (dotted line), according to Ryan and Pitman, superimposed on the current Black Sea. The dotted line conforms fairly well to the 100m (328ft) isobath. Redrawn from the Wikipedia article on the deluge theory.

a much smaller area than it covers today (see Fig 21). At the same time, the theory goes, the general levels of the earth's seas were rising following the ending of the ice ages. Eventually, the Mediterranean rose to such an extent that it eventually spilled over the rocky shallow sill in what we now call the Bosphorus and cascaded into the Black Sea basin. According to Ryan and Pitman, 42 cubic kilometres (10 cubic miles) of water flowed over the sill each day – 200 times the flow over Niagara Falls – eventually extending the area of the Black Sea by some 155,000 square kilometres (60,000 square miles), particularly to the north and west, that is, into the Sea of Azov and around the Crimean peninsula. Since humans were certainly living in the area at the time, it is suggested that this dramatic and potentially catastrophic event could well have given rise to the Noah's flood story.

Although there is no doubt that the connection between the Black Sea and the Mediterranean was broken from time to time in the geological past, there is considerable controversy among scientists about the relative levels of the two water bodies and the speed at which any flow from one to the other occurred. And there is also doubt about whether humans were living on the shores of the postulated reduced Black Sea at the time. Almost inevitably, the problem attracted the attention of American geologist Robert Ballard, who achieved world fame in the 1980s for his work on the wreck of the RMS *Titanic*. In a series of expeditions to the Black Sea led by Ballard, marine archaeologists recovered a variety of evidence of human activity close to ancient shorelines at depths of some 100m (330ft) off the northern coast of modern Turkey, though the carbon dating of some of the artefacts does not fit terribly well with the 5,600BC timescale. Nevertheless, it is an intriguing thought that a world-shattering natural event some 7,500 years ago might have been witnessed by some of our ancestors, providing the basis for a story that has been handed down from generation to generation to the present day.

40 Where and what is the Sargasso Sea?

Sargasso Sea is the name given to a huge area of the central North Atlantic Ocean, famed for its accumulation of floating seaweed. Instead of the shorelines that border most seas, the boundaries of the Sargasso Sea are the major surface currents of the North Atlantic Gyre (see Q70)[52]. Its boundaries are therefore a bit hazy, but broadly it extends some 3,000km (1,865 miles) between the Canary Islands in the east and Bermuda in the west, and about 1,000km (620 miles) from a bit south of the Azores in the north to a latitude of about 25°N – that is, about level with Miami, Florida (see Fig 22).

The regions between about 25° and 40° north and south of the equator in all the oceans are typified by long periods of calm with little or no wind. They are sometimes referred to collectively as the 'horse latitudes', a term said to have been applied in the days of sail initially to this region in the North Atlantic – that is, the Sargasso Sea. The derivation of the name is uncertain, but there are at least two possible explanations, both based on the difficulties in traversing these regions experienced by sailing vessels in the absence of wind. One rather unlikely explanation[53] suggests that it refers to the fact that seamen transporting horses from Europe to North America and the West Indies often had to jettison their cargo because their passage had been delayed to the point where they could no longer feed or water the animals. A marginally less implausible explanation[54] says that it is based on the curious use of the term 'dead horse' by sailors to refer to the period at the beginning of a voyage, usually a month, for which they had been paid in advance (and possibly spent the

---

52   These boundary currents are the north and north-easterly flowing Gulf Stream in the west, the easterly North Atlantic Current in the north, the south-westerly Canaries Current in the east and the westerly North Equatorial in the south.
53   See WH Smyth's *The Sailor's Word-Book*, first published in 1867 and reissued by Conway Maritime Press in 1991.
54   See *The Oxford Companion to Ships and the Sea*, edited by Peter Kemp and published in 1976.

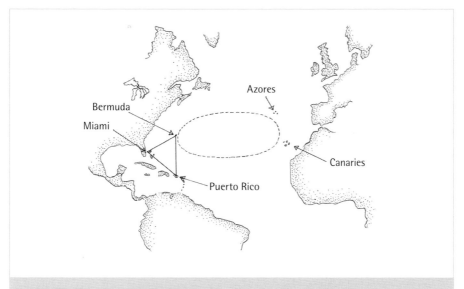

Figure 22
The North Atlantic Ocean, showing the positions of the Sargasso Sea (broken line) and the Bermuda Triangle (solid line).

money). The 'dead horse' had to be worked off before they were due for further pay. This event (ie pay day) was so important that a custom developed of parading a straw-stuffed effigy of a horse around the deck before eventually throwing it overboard. Since this ceremony often took place with the ship still becalmed in the windless region of the Atlantic, it became known as the horse latitudes.[55]

However, the name Sargasso Sea for the region is a good deal older, and comes from the word *salgazo*, the Portuguese term for a particular small variety of grape. Early sailors crossing the Atlantic, possibly even those with Columbus, were reminded of these tiny grapes by the small gas-filled bladders supporting great rafts of floating seaweed that they encountered in the central Atlantic. Odd patches of seaweeds are found floating at the surface in many areas of the world's oceans particularly relatively close to land. Almost invariably, these clumps have been ripped by rough weather from their normal habitat attached to rocks in fairly shallow water. But they are particularly abundant in the Sargasso Sea for two reasons. First, the combination of major currents around the region and minor

55   This is also possibly the derivation of the expression 'to flog a dead horse', originally meaning that any attempt to get seamen to do extra work while they were still working off their advanced pay was a fruitless task, doomed to failure!

currents within it tend to accumulate any floating material in the area, unfortunately including polluting junk like plastic bags and beer cans[56]. Second, however,
at least two species of seaweed, *Sargassum natans* and *Sargassum fluitans*, have
broken with the normal lifestyle of their relatives anchored to the seabed and
have opted instead for a fully floating existence (see Fig 23), growing and repro-
ducing entirely out of contact with any hard surface. It was the small, gas-filled
floats of the sargassum weeds, standing on little stalks, that reminded the Portuguese sailors of grapes and prompted the name.

It is estimated that, at any one time, there may be between 4 and 11 million
metric tonnes of floating weed in the Sargasso Sea. In the days of sailing ships,
the masses of vegetation were considered a serious threat to shipping since they
were thought capable of completely halting a vessel in its tracks. Nowadays, this
is not a significant problem and the weed masses are usually considered in a more
positive light. First, there is a small, but significant, industry based on harvesting
the weed for use either as fertiliser or in the manufacture of soaps and skin creams.
Second, the weed clumps are the basis of a whole community of animals, particularly crustaceans (shrimps and crabs) and fishes, some of which are found only
in this unusual environment. Furthermore, many oceanic fishes, including the
juveniles of game fishes such as marlin, billfishes and swordfish, use the weed
patches as refuges to escape from potential natural predators – only to fall victim
in their maturity to the ultimate predator, the sport fisherman!

Figure 23
A patch of sargassum weed photographed in the North Atlantic in January 2010.

56   See also Q74 dealing with the Great Pacific Garbage Patch.

41 Is there really such a thing as the Bermuda Triangle?

The Bermuda Triangle, also sometimes known as the Devil's Triangle, is an area of the western North Atlantic in which a number of ships and aircraft are alleged to have disappeared under mysterious circumstances. Different authors and commentators specify a range of boundaries for the area, but the commonest definition seems to be the triangle bordered by lines joining Miami, Bermuda and Puerto Rico (see Fig 22).

This general region is renowned for its violent thunderstorms and waterspouts, and Christopher Columbus commented on its bad weather when he sailed through the area in the early months of 1493. However, it did not achieve its current notoriety until the 1950s when several newspaper and magazine articles were published, particularly in the USA, suggesting that there had been a number of unexplained losses of ships and planes in the general area of Bermuda.

The main stimulus to these reports was the loss of 'Flight 19', a group of five TBM torpedo bomber aircraft on a training mission from US Naval Air Station Fort Lauderdale in Florida on 5 December 1945. All five planes disappeared without trace, with the loss of 14 airmen on the flight. Later the same day a PBM Mariner flying boat was also lost, along with its crew of 13, while searching for the missing bombers. Although neither incident has been satisfactorily explained, there is reasonable evidence that the flying boat exploded in mid air, presumably as a result of a catastrophic systems failure. But the loss of Flight 19 is more controversial, particularly because in the Navy's own accident report it was attributed to 'causes or reasons unknown', though the most likely explanation is human error on the part of the leading pilot.

Whatever the true explanations for these losses, the articles written about them resulted in a huge amount of interest and the rapid development of a widely held belief that there was something very mysterious in the area leading to the disappearances. In support of these ideas, its adherents began compiling lists of other supposedly unexplained losses in the area[57], and an equally impressive list of possible explanations ranging from weird local effects on compasses, through rogue waves (see *Do Whales...?* 102) and methane 'burps' (see Q44) to supernatural forces or UFOs[58].

As a result, the last 60 years have seen the appearance of dozens of articles, books, films and television programmes, either in support of the idea that the area

---

57   The list of 'unexplained' events range from the loss of the US Naval vessel *Grampus* off Charleston in
       1843 to the mysterious disappearance of two lighthouse keepers from the Great Isaac Lighthouse on
       the island of Bimini in the Bahamas in 1969.
58   See, for instance, Steven Spielberg's 1977 film *Close Encounters of the Third Kind.*

has some sinister secret or attempting to debunk it. Unfortunately for the fans of such mysteries, the available hard evidence seems to be stacked against the Bermuda Triangle being any different from lots of other parts of the world ocean, at least as far as ship and plane losses are concerned. For example, the marine insurers Lloyds of London (see Q64) (who should certainly know what they are talking about, since losses cost them money) say that the area is not characterised by an unusually large number of ship losses. Even more damning, the US Coast Guard suggest that, in view of the very large number of ships and aircraft regularly passing through the area, the reported losses are relatively few compared with other areas. But as we all know, few journalists let inconvenient facts get in the way of a good story – so I expect the Bermuda Triangle and the folklore that has grown up around it will live on for many a long year.

42 What is the deep sea floor made of?

Underneath all the deep ocean basins there is a layer of hard rock, several kilometres thick, called the oceanic crust or lithosphere. This material is produced at sea floor spreading centres or axes (see *Do Whales...?* Q22), including the mid-ocean ridges (see *Do Whales...?* Q17), where it may be exposed and therefore form the actual bed of the ocean. Continental or land-derived rock may also be exposed on the bed of the shallow Continental Shelves or on the steepest parts of the Continental Slope.

However, the bedrock under most of the oceans is overlain by blankets of soft sediments, often many kilometres thick. Some of these sediments are gravels, sands and muds derived from the weathering and erosion of land areas and carried to the ocean by rivers, glaciers and wind. Although small amounts of this terrestrial material can be found almost anywhere in the oceans, it forms a significant proportion of the seabed sediment only in a few restricted ocean margin areas, particularly around the borders of the North Atlantic. In the same way, volcanic ash and pumice can be found in small amounts all over the ocean, but is significant only fairly close to the volcanic sources such as mid-oceanic volcanic islands.

In contrast, the vast majority of the deep sea floor sediments are made up of billions of tiny fragments of the skeletal remains of countless marine plants and animals that have died and sunk to the seabed over the last 150 million years or so, forming muds known by the wonderfully descriptive term 'ooze'. Deep-sea oozes fall into two main classes, dominated respectively either by chalky (calcium carbonate) or glass-like (siliceous) material. Although both materials are found all over the deep ocean, the calcareous material dominates the sediments in the slightly shallower parts, while it tends to dissolve under the high pressures of the deepest oceans, leaving the sediments dominated by glassy material.

Chalky sediments are made up mainly of the remains of one group of tiny plants, the coccolithophores (see *Do Whales...?* Q27), and two animal groups, the foraminiferans (see Q5) and the pteropods, strange little swimming snails (see *Do Whales...?* Q40). Similarly, the glassy sediments come from both plants (the diatoms, see *Do Whales...?* Q27) and animals (the radiolarians, see Q5).

The plants and animals that produced these remains lived mainly in mid-water as part of the plankton. Depending on how productive the waters were, the sediments beneath them accumulated at rates between about 1mm and 10cm every thousand years, with a mean of about 3cm (1in). This process is still going on today, of course, and the surface few centimetres of the deep sea floor, laid down in the last few years, tends to be very soft and flocculent mud, easily disturbed by the various animals that burrow into it, crawl and slither across it or swim over it. However, 20 or 30cm (8–12in) down, the weight of the sediment deposited on top compacts the tiny particles and squeezes out much of the water so that the mud becomes rather firm and almost dry, despite the vast amount of water above it.

But despite the surface layers being churned up and therefore 'blurred', the sedimentary column preserves a record of past changes in the overlying water that can be unravelled by oceanographers. By collecting long cores of bottom mud and examining changes in the relative proportions of species whose shells make it up and details of the sediment and interstitial water chemistry, marine scientists can determine what the ocean was like tens or hundreds of thousands of years ago.

Of course, these natural materials are not the only things to be found on the deep sea floor, and there is ample evidence of man's impact on even the most remote ocean areas. Nowadays there are strict controls on the dumping of material from ships of all the main maritime nations (see Q62), but for hundreds of years it was the accepted way of getting rid of waste at sea. Consequently, the sea floor is littered with bottles and cans, bits of pottery and all sorts of synthetic materials like plastic bags, netting and even cocktail sticks.

However, perhaps the most abundant and widespread evidence of man's maritime activities is clinker, the unburned residues from the fireboxes of coal-fired steam vessels. In my own experience, not one of the dozens of trawl samples I saw brought up from the bottom of the deep sea was without at least some clinker, if only a few small fragments, the vast majority having been dumped within about a hundred years from 1850 to 1950.

On the other hand, some artefacts brought up from the bottom were much more welcome. The best of these were about a dozen small spherical objects, each about a centimetre in diameter, dredged from the bottom of the Bay of Biscay. They turned out to be made of lead and were clearly 18th-century musket balls, almost certainly British, French or Dutch. It doesn't take an Einstein to guess that they were probably also fired at sailors belonging to one or other of these nationalities, presumably falling short of their target and sinking to their final resting place several kilometres below. What a tale they could tell if only we could decipher it!

43 What are manganese nodules?

Manganese nodules, more properly called polymetallic nodules, are metal-rich pebble-like objects found in various localities on the deep sea floor.

They were first discovered in the North Atlantic in 1873 by the British naval vessel HMS *Challenger,* dredging in very deep water to the south-west of the Canary Islands. Since that time they have been found in many parts of the world ocean and are particularly abundant on the floor of the central Pacific, in an area known as the Clipperton-Clarion Fracture Zone or CCFZ. In this region the nodules may be so abundant that they are almost touching one another on the seabed.

The nodules are typically brown to black-coloured, potato-shaped lumps ranging in size from less than 1cm (0.39in) in diameter to about 25cm (10in) across, with surface textures ranging from smooth to quite rough and gritty. These differences apparently reflect different origins and rates of production, for the nodules are believed to have been formed by the accretion (like precipitation) of metallic salts from the surrounding seawater over long periods of time. Nodule growth rates are usually estimated to have been of the order of a few millimetres per million years, so that the largest nodules must be many millions of years old. A bit like a pearl inside an oyster shell, all manganese nodules have a nucleus of some sort onto which the first salts were deposited. These nuclei can be almost anything from tiny bits of clay, fragments of pumice (from the outpourings of volcanoes), sponge spicules or fish bones. Most spectacularly, quite a few nodules have prehistoric sharks' teeth at their centre.

Among the many remarkable features of manganese nodules is that, despite their great age, they are invariably found at the very surface of the seabed sediments, lying half buried and half exposed to the overlying water. Why they remain at the surface in this way, and are not covered by the rain of tiny particles constantly falling onto the sea floor from the water column, is something of a mystery. It is assumed that deep-sea animals crawling across or under the sediments nudge the nodules from time to time and prevent sediment from accumulating on top of them.

Apart from their scientific interest, manganese nodules have a huge economic potential because of their metal content. Nodule chemistry varies from place to place, but can include a wide range of valuable metals such as gold, silver, platinum, titanium, molybdenum and zinc. But these constituents are usually in such small concentrations that they would not justify the costs of mining. On the other hand, the amounts of copper, cobalt, nickel and manganese present in many nodules have attracted the attention of industry and even national governments because of their potential as a source of raw materials if the more conventional land-based sources become less attractive for economic or political reasons. Consequently, a number of claims to mining rights to areas of the CCFZ have already been regis-tered with the International Seabed Authority of the United Nations, particularly on behalf of the USA and Russia.

Since these claims are mainly in water depths of 4,000 to 6,000m (13,000–20,000ft), the technology required to recover the nodules and separate them from the surrounding sediment is both expensive and extremely complex. As a result, the estimated scale of operation that would be necessary to justify the investment is mind-boggling.

Even in the richest areas, where an average of 10kg (22lb) of nodules can be expected on every square metre (11 square ft) of sea floor, something like 1.5 million metric tonnes would have to be mined each year for a minimum of 20 years to make it economically viable. This would mean mining about 1 km^2 (0.3 square miles) of sea floor every working day or about 6,000 km^2 (2,300 square miles) over the 20-year period. Apart from the impact of such an activity on the seabed, the environmental consequences of the mud cloud that would inevitably be produced is rather worrying.

Between 1974 and 1982, governments and private companies spent more than 1 billion US dollars on manganese nodule investigations. None of these endeavours became commercially successful, mainly because the high costs of collection and extraction were not matched by the costs of the metals available from other sources. However, interest in deep-sea mining has been stimulated in recent years by the rapidly increasing price of metals, particularly of gold and copper, resulting from the huge demands of the 'new' economies like China, India and Brazil. This interest is likely to wane a bit during the current world recession, but will undoubt-edly pick up again within a few years. When it does so, attention in the short term is likely to focus on so-called sea-floor massive sulphide (SMS) deposits recently identified in various parts of the deep sea floor.

These sulphide deposits may be formed whenever cold seawater comes into contact with hot rocks. This can happen around submarine volcanoes at the margins of tectonic plates, but the deposits are also particularly well developed at hydro-thermal vents centred on the mid-oceanic ridge system and usually at depths between about 1,500 and 3,500m (5,000–11,500ft) – that is, a good deal shallower than most manganese nodule fields. As described in *Do Whales...?* Q18, the vents themselves – cracks and holes in the sea floor, through which very hot water gushes – are usually restricted to a few tens, or at most hundreds, of square metres. But the water for these hot springs originates from a much wider area, possibly extending several hundreds of metres away from the vents. Over this broad area, cold seawater – usually at a temperature of no more than 2–4°C (36–39°F) – seeps down into the sea floor through cracks and fissures in the sediments and underlying rocks, sometimes to a depth of some hundreds of metres. As it sinks it is heated up by the hot magma under the relatively thin crust and the hot water then reacts with the rocks through which it is percolating. In the process, the water loses its oxygen, becomes more acidic, and picks up high concentrations of metals, particularly iron, manganese, copper, zinc and lead. But it may also accumulate traces of much more precious metals such as gold, silver and platinum.

Eventually this metal-laden hot water becomes so buoyant that it begins to rise up through the sediments, ultimately to spew out of the sea floor as the now familiar hot 'fountains'. If it makes this vertical journey through the sediments without encountering any cold, oxygenated water on the way, it emerges at a very high temperature of 350°C (660°F) or even more. The resulting stream of billowing water will be full of black or brown particles, mainly of metallic sulphides, but also including oxides and hydroxides. The emerging column of water looks very like smoke so that, not surprisingly, these vents are called 'black smokers'. But there is another good reason for the name. As the hot water suddenly hits the cold oxygenated water immediately above the sea floor, it deposits some of its load of metal sulphides as circular 'chimneys', which can grow to impressive structures tens of metres tall before they eventually topple under their own weight, to start the process all over again.

Fascinating though these black smokers are to oceanographers and marine biologists, they are not the ones that are likely to be attractive to metal prospectors. Instead, it will be another class of vents, the so-called white smokers, that will receive their attention. As the name suggests, the water gushing from white smokers is much paler than that from black smokers, though in truth it is usually a rather dirty grey colour rather than white. And the reason is that, unlike the black smokers, this water mixed with cold oxygenated water as it rose up through the sediments. The result is not only that the emerging water is a good deal cooler than black smoker water (though still at an impressive 200°C/390°F or so), but it is much less laden with chemical – hence the colour. White smokers also tend not to produce the huge chimneys characteristic of black smokers. Instead, much of the chemical load will have been left behind in the sediments as sulphide deposits, those so far found ranging from a few thousand tonnes to around 100 million tones and enriched with copper, zinc, lead and cadmium, as well as with gold and silver.

Although no commercial deep-sea mining for metals has yet started, a number of organizations are already actively involved in planning for the possibility. In particular, two companies – Nautilus Minerals and Neptune Minerals (unsurprising names!) – have been especially active and are now quoted on the London Stock Exchange. Both companies are concentrating on the south-western Pacific region, a tectonically very active region running through New Zealand, north to Tonga and Fiji and then north-westwards to Papua New Guinea before turning north to run past the islands of Japan (basically following the western edge of the Pacific tectonic plate, see *Do Whales…?* Q22). Between them, the two companies already have licenses to explore, and possibly exploit, deposits over an area of almost one million square kilometres of seabed. Pilot mining operations are in an advanced state of planning and fully commercial operations are likely to start within a few years. Because of the potential environmental impact of these activities, particularly on the unique communities associated with hydrothermal vents, there will be close scrutiny of the operations by environmental groups and by the International Seabed Authority of the International Maritime Organization (see Q71).

44 What are methane clathrates?

Methane clathrates, also called gas hydrates, are strange mixtures of natural gas and water in which the gas molecules are trapped in a sort of icy meshwork of water molecules with a consistency a bit like a sorbet[59].

Methane clathrates form under rather special circumstances, either in the permafrost beneath cold land areas or in deep-sea sediments, both situations being made possible by high pressures and low temperatures. When their existence beneath the oceans was first recognised in the 1960s and 70s it was thought that they might occur throughout the entire ocean floor. However, we now know that they can form only in a fairly narrow range of depths between about 300 and 500m (1,000–1,650ft) – that is, on the outer edges of the continental shelves. Nevertheless, significant gas-bearing sediments have been found, or have been inferred with a high degree of confidence, in many locations around the world. Although the gas is usually in rather low concentrations, current estimates suggest that somewhere between 1×10^{15} and 5×10^{15} (that is 1–5 quadrillion) cubic metres of methane is locked up in the world's clathrates. This is between about two and ten times the currently estimated reserves of conventional natural gas. It is clearly a potentially very valuable resource, though the development of the technology to extract it safely and efficiently is still in the early stages.

Because of their relative volatility, clathrates have been, and still are, regarded with a degree of ambivalence. Until fairly recently, oil and gas geologists usually

59   The name 'clathrate' is derived from the Latin word *clathratus*, meaning 'meshwork' or 'lattice'.

considered them a bit of a nuisance when they chanced upon them because they caused inconvenient blowouts and blocked pipelines. Methane is also recognised as a particularly powerful greenhouse gas; in fact, 20 times more powerful molecule for molecule in warming the atmosphere than the usual climate-change *bête noire*, carbon dioxide. So the last thing we want in a warming world is for the methane in clathrates to be released willy-nilly into the atmosphere[60].

In their normal situation, most clathrates seem to be reasonably stable, though they can be disturbed, and some clathrates certainly have been from time to time in the past. For example, the Storegga Slide, a huge mass of sediment on the floor of the deep ocean to the west of Norway, broke away from the Norwegian continental shelf some 8,000 years ago, causing an underwater landslide of something like 3,500 km³ (840 cubic miles) of debris and a tsunami that would have affected large areas of the north-eastern Atlantic. Although it is possible that the triggering event was a submarine earthquake, a major contributory effect would have been the release of gas from huge gas hydrate deposits typical of this region, then and now.

Natural releases of gas from clathrates have also been implicated in sudden sinkings of vessels, for example in the Bemuda Triangle area (see Q41). These ideas are based on laboratory experiments in which gas bubbles released in water tanks beneath ship models have reduced the density of the water to such an extent that it would no longer support the models, which promptly sank. So far there are no reliable reports of this sort of thing happening in nature.

45 Why is there oil and gas under the sea floor?

The dreadful events surrounding the explosion on BP's Deepwater Horizon drilling platform in the Gulf of Mexico in the spring of 2010 caused tragic loss of life and the worst maritime environmental impact to hit the USA. It brought into question the whole ethos of deep-sea drilling for oil and/or gas and whether the risks

---

60   In March 2010, scientists from the University of Alaska, Fairbanks, reported that analysis of seawater and atmospheric samples over the East Siberian Arctic Shelf (or ESAS) indicate that methane is currently leaking from the sea floor at an estimated rate of some 7 million tonnes each year – that is, only about one fiftieth of the total annual emission of methane to the atmosphere. This ESAS methane is not from clathrates, but from permafrost now forming part of the seabed at depths not much more than about 50m. The permafrost was produced when the present sea floor in the region was last exposed above sea level, but no one knows whether the release of methane in the region has been going on for a long time or is a recent phenomenon and, perhaps, related to global warming. If it is caused by global warming, then the discovery raises the fear that much larger amounts of methane may be released as the Arctic seas get warmer and will simply add to the greenhouse problem!

involved in these undertakings are worth it. But it also highlighted the more general question about why it is that so much of the earth's oil and gas deposits seem to lie deep beneath the ocean?

Oil and gas are hydrocarbons – that is, chemical compounds made up of hydrogen and carbon atoms, often linked together in long chains. Almost all naturally occurring oil and gas is derived from the remains of plants and animals decaying under special conditions, usually buried deep underground where there is no oxygen and they are basically 'cooked' under high temperatures and pressures. Under these circumstances, terrestrial plant remains are usually converted into coal (at fairly shallow depths) and gas (if buried more deeply). Some undersea gas has been derived in this way but most submarine oil and gas deposits were derived from an aquatic origin. For example, the huge reserves under the northern North Sea and in areas like the Gulf of Mexico were derived from the remains of prehistoric bacteria and tiny planktonic plants and animals living in lakes and shallow seas. For this material to produce oil reservoirs such as those we exploit today, three conditions had to be met.

First, the sediments made up of the plant and animal debris had to be buried deeply enough under other geological layers for the material to be exposed to sufficiently high temperatures and pressures to cook it. With increasing depth, both temperature and pressure increase. The initial effect is to make the fats, waxes and oils in the organic material link up to form a sort of oil precursor, called kerogen. With increasing depth and higher temperatures and pressures, the kerogen is converted successively, first into a very waxy and thick heavy oil consisting of long hydrocarbon chains, next into rather shorter chain light oil, and finally into gas. Oil forms under the North Sea at about 3–4.5km (2–3 mile) depth and gas at 4–6km (2½–4 mile) depth.

Once the oil or gas has been produced, it will migrate away from the source rock into permeable layers that act more or less like a sponge and hold the hydrocarbons in the spaces between the rock or sediment particles. So the second requirement for an oil or gas reservoir is for a suitable nearby porous reservoir rock where it can accumulate.

Finally, to stop the oil and gas escaping into the overlying air or water, an impermeable layer or cap is needed to cover the reservoir and hold it in place for millions of years until the oilman comes to drill through it and extract the 'black gold'. Without any one of these three elements there is no hope of an exploitable resource, so the oil geologist must find good evidence of this unique combination before any oil company will risk the huge expense of a trial drilling.

Of course, tapping into these reserves is a very risky business, as the Deepwater Horizon story so graphically demonstrated; for if the impermeable layer over the top of an oil or gas reservoir is penetrated in any way, either naturally through normal geological processes, or artificially by a drill string, the contents will be forced by the pressure within the reservoir to spill out into the sea. For the oilman this is the dreaded 'blowout', and it seems to have been a problem with the blowout preventer, a sort of high-tech plug, that led to the terrible explosion, tragic loss of life and subsequent massive leak from Deepwater Horizon. But appalling though the effects of the oil were on the local wildlife and the livelihood of the people living in the area, it was by no means a unique incident. Most of us have heard of, or can even remember, the dreadful tanker oil spills from the *Exxon Valdez* off Alaska in 1989 and the *Torrey Canyon* off the coast of Cornwall in 1967. Both of these were extreme examples, though neither of them comparing with the Deepwater Horizon spill. But hundreds of much smaller spills have occurred in various parts of the world from drilling platforms or from tankers over the last hundred years or so. And thousand upon thousand of natural seeps must have occurred over geological time, as they are still doing today on dry land in many parts of the world. So countless millions of tonnes of oil and gas must have sloshed around the seas over the aeons. Not surprisingly, this has resulted in the evolution of whole communities of tiny organisms, mainly bacteria, able to thrive on the hydrocarbons and break them down into simpler harmless substances like water and CO_2. The bacterial growth is then fed on by other organisms, resulting in rich seabed communities a bit like those around hydrothermal vents (see *Do Whales...?* Q18), totally independent of photosynthesis, the process that supports the vast majority of life on earth and in the oceans. Curiously, in view of the huge problems surrounding the Deepwater Horizon affair, probably the best known of these so-called cold seep communities is only a few miles away from the BP well site, on the Louisiana continental slope where US scientists have been studying them for many years. Experience of dealing with previous major spills, particularly going back to the *Torrey Canyon* over 40 years ago, suggests that trying to disperse the oil using chemicals can sometimes do more severe and longer-lasting damage to the ecosystem than letting nature largely get on with the job.

46 What is the SOFAR channel?

The SOFAR (Sound Fixing and Ranging) Channel is a horizontal layer in the ocean that acts as a particularly efficient conduit for low frequency sound waves.

Sound travels through water about five times as fast as it travels through air, roughly at 1,500m (5,000ft) a second. But the precise speed in seawater varies from about 1,480 to 1,550m (4,855–5,085ft) per second depending upon the temperature, pressure and salinity.

The SOFAR channel is centred around the depth where the speed of sound is at a minimum, relatively close to the surface at high latitudes (beyond 60°N and 60°S) and at depths down to about 1,000m (3,280ft) or more in tropical regions. Sound waves that deviate from the channel, either shallower or deeper, begin to travel faster and are refracted back towards the centre of the channel. Consequently, waves within the channel follow a path oscillating across the channel axis, but travelling much further before dissipating than sounds propagated outside the channel.

The channel is important in submarine warfare, but is also thought to be exploited by whales, particularly humpbacks, to communicate over very long distances.

47 Why should oceanographers be interested in rubber ducks?

Basically, because they float and are carried along by water currents. So if you know where and when they got into the sea, and where they were picked up, they can tell you a lot about the surface currents. And not just rubber ducks, of course, but almost anything that floats. In fact, the first direct evidence for the existence of the Gulf Stream, linking the Caribbean with Europe, came in 1696 when Hans Sloane, whose personal collections formed the basis of the British Museum, realised that the large sea beans[61] frequently found on the shores of western Ireland and Scotland originated from trees he had seen growing in Jamaica.

Using the same principle, shipwrecked mariners have traditionally thrown bottles containing desperate messages into the sea in the hope that they would be carried by ocean currents to some friendly shore, where they would be picked up by a potential rescuer. But the very first recorded messages in bottles were apparently those thrown into the Mediterranean by the philosopher Theophrastus in around 310BC in an attempt to prove that water came into the sea through the Strait of Gibraltar. There is no record as to whether any of his bottles were found, but the same technique, using bottles with printed messages inside them, was widely used by oceanographers and fishery scientists during the 20th century to try to trace ocean currents. The messages inside the bottles, usually in several languages, would offer a small reward for anyone who discovered the bottle and let the experimenter know where and when it was found. Because of the costs involved, typically no

---

61   Sometimes known as goblins' kidneys on account of their shape.

more than a few hundred bottles would be released in a single experiment and the number reported within a reasonable time would rarely represent more than a few per cent. Nevertheless, over many years – and lots of experiments – the technique yielded plenty of information that, at the time, could not have been obtained in any other way.

With the developments in technology – particularly the use of electronics and satellite technology in the second half of the century – much more sophisticated techniques for studying surface currents were developed. Nevertheless, the old floating bottle technique was still used from time to time, but was always hampered by the very low return rate relative to the expense of the bottles. Imagine, then, the delight of scientists studying the surface circulation of the Pacific Ocean when they were provided with a 'drift bottle' experiment that cost them absolutely nothing to set up.

The scientists involved were Curtis Ebbesmeyer and James Ingraham, two Seattle oceanographers who had already been tracing the paths of various bits and pieces accidentally or intentionally dropped in the ocean to help with their mathematical models of the Pacific's surface currents. But these paled into insignificance beside two chance events in the early 1990s.

The first, in May 1990, involved the release not of ducks, rubber or otherwise, but of some 60,000 Nike shoes instead! The shoes were being transported from Korea to the USA in the Hansa Shipping Company container ship *Hansa Carrier,* when she encountered a severe storm in the North Pacific at about 48°N 161°W, some 1,700nm north of Hawaii. During the storm, 21 containers were washed overboard, five of them filled with about 80,000 Nike shoes ranging from children's footwear to hiking boots. It was later estimated that four of the containers burst open, releasing more than 60,000 shoes into the ocean. The model used by Ebbesmeyer and Ingraham predicted that the shoes would be carried to Vancouver Island and the central coast of British Columbia in about 250 days – and the first reports did, indeed, come from Vancouver Island about 220 days after the spill. Eventually, Ebbesmeyer was able to account for some 1,300 shoes found on a range of Pacific beaches, including some carried as far as Hawaii via the coasts of Washington, Oregon and California. Of course, not too surprisingly considering the popularity of the Nike brand, lots of the shoes found on beaches had not come from the *Hansa Carrier.* However, Ebbesmeyer was able to eliminate these because of the unique serial number on the spilled consignment that the manufacturers were able to give him.

Amazingly, two years after the Nike shoe affair, Ebbesmeyer was presented with another free 'experiment', this time with children's plastic bath toys, known as *Friendly Floatees,* manufactured in China and marketed in the USA by The First Years, Inc. These toys included red beavers, green frogs, blue turtles and, yes, yellow ducks. Like the Nike shoes, they were being transported in containers, this time from Hong Kong to Tacoma, Washington. On 10 January 1992, when the ship carrying them was close to the International Dateline (at about 45°N 178°E), 12 containers were washed overboard in a storm, one of them containing no less than 29,000 *Friendly Floatees*. As before, the container broke open and released the toys into the ocean to drift where the winds and currents took them.

The first reports of landfalls came ten months later, on 16 November 1992, when six were found just south of Sitka, Alaska, and several hundreds more were reported during the next few months, also mainly from Alaskan shores. The resulting data allowed Ebbesmeyer and Ingraham to refine their model and make predictions about where they might turn up over the ensuing few years. These predictions suggested that at least some of the toys would be carried north, through the Bering Sea and into the Arctic Ocean, possibly to emerge some five years or so later into the waters of the North Atlantic.

By the year 2000 they had, indeed, made it into the Atlantic, being recorded on various shores from Maine to Massachusetts, and by 2003 they had even reached the Hebrides. The models suggested that they should reach the shores of southern Britain by 2007 and, spot on cue, in July 2007 a lady walking her dog found one on the Devon coast. Unfortunately, this one turned out not to have come from the Pacific consignment; a particular shame for the lady who found it, because genuine ones have become collectors' items and change hands at anything up to $1,000 dollars. So keep your eyes open when walking along any beach!

IV
Fishing

Do Whales...? included virtually nothing about the exploitation of the oceans in general or fishing in particular, mainly because of lack of space. This time I have no such excuse, and although the topic is dealt with much more adequately in recent books like those by Charles Clover, Philip Hoare and Calum Roberts, all included in the reference list, I've tackled a few of the most basic questions like how much fish do we, could we or should we take from the oceans – and why. I've also referred to a few of the organisations with responsibility in some or all of these areas. Brief though they are, they will hopefully whet your appetite to find out more about these crucial topics.

48 How much fish do we take from the oceans?

This is not an easy question to answer. Even the ultimate authority on the subject, the Food and Agriculture Organisation (FAO) of the United Nations, admits that its statistics are a touch flaky, and particularly the numbers coming out of China, now by far the biggest fishing nation on earth. Nevertheless, it is possible to have a pretty good stab at an answer, at least up to the year 2000, the last one for which full figures are available.

At that time, the total world fish catch[62] was estimated at 94.8 million tonnes, the bulk of it (86 million tonnes) coming from the oceans and 8.8 million tonnes

---

62   In this context, the word 'fish' includes shellfish.

from 'inland waters' – that is, freshwater rivers and lakes and landlocked seas such as the Caspian. These figures had hovered around more or less the same levels for the previous decade; but during the preceding 40 years they had grown astronomically, the total catch figure rising from about 20 million tonnes in 1950 to 90 million tonnes in 1990. During the same period, while the total fish catch had increased by a factor of about 4.5, the world human population had approximately doubled from about 2.52 billion in 1950 to just over 5 billion in 1990. So the fish catch had more than kept up with the population growth, the annual catch per person in 1950 being about 8kg (18lb), rising to 17kg (35lb) in 1990 – wonderful, particularly if you are fond of fish! But since that time the situation has changed dramatically. While the total catch has remained more or less static, the world population has grown inexorably. By the year 2000 the world population was estimated at 6.1 billion, so that the catch per person had fallen to 15kg (33lb). Sadly, this situation is likely to get much worse, because while we are unlikely to get through the 100 million tonne annual catch barrier despite our best, or worst, efforts, the fish-hungry world population will almost certainly carry on growing, possibly doubling again by mid-century!

So why can't we catch more fish? Well, you don't have to be an Einstein to work it out. With rare exceptions, pretty well all traditional fisheries, including those around Europe and the North Atlantic generally, have been overfished for the best part of a century or more. Overfishing is a complex subject, but basically it means taking more out of a population than it is capable of replacing on a long-term basis. The effects are obvious. First, the fish get more difficult to catch, so to capture the same amount takes more and more fishing effort; for the consumer, the effect is that the price goes up. Second, the average size of the animals captured goes down. Initially, this simply reduces the number of very old animals in the population, but eventually it means that more and more animals are being captured before they are old enough to reproduce, with the inevitable result that there are fewer youngsters being born. Finally, the target species becomes so rare that it is impossible for fishermen to make a living from catching them and the fishery collapses.

This scenario has been repeated time after time in various parts of the world, including the Mediterranean, the North Sea and the North Atlantic, despite all sorts of measures like catch quotas, net mesh size regulations, no-go areas, close seasons and so on. So how on earth did the total world catch increase so much between 1950 and 1990? Essentially, by a combination of two quite different developments. First, by exploiting previously unfished species or unfished areas, and second, by increasingly efficient fishing technology enabling fishing companies to continue to make profits allowing apparently economic exploitation even as the fished populations become more and more depleted. But both of these strategies have limits.

Improving technology is all very well, but it can't conjure up target fish when they are not there, and this has certainly happened to the herring fisheries around north-western Europe and the cod fisheries in the North Atlantic. Similarly, new areas and new target species may well initially provide a bonanza for the exploiting fishermen, but they are often based on species that would previously have been discarded because they were considered either too small to land or of inferior quality. So their market value is often relatively low. And even if the quality is fine, these newly exploited fisheries can rapidly collapse if the populations are hit too hard, particularly if this is done without regard to their biology. For a classic example of bad management of a new fishery in recent decades look at Q29 on the orange roughy.

The sad, but perhaps inevitable lesson from all this is that the bountiful sea may not be quite as bountiful as many people would like to think. Certainly, the history of man's use of the living resources of the oceans – whether of cod, mussels or squid, and seals or whales – is littered with examples of over-exploitation and disaster. Rarely, if ever, do we seem to learn from our mistakes. Fortunately, and hopefully not too late, the situation is beginning to change and there is a growing body of international opinion insisting that our attitude to the oceans and their resources must change[63]. Look at the questions on aquaculture and marine reserves for a slightly more optimistic story.

Furthermore, there is an alternative view suggesting that if we organised things better we might be able not only to sustain the present fish catch, but even increase it. Wow!

In 2009 the World Bank published the results of a study of the current state of world fisheries, carried out by an Icelandic economist and two FAO[64] fisheries biologists, along with estimates of what might be possible if we fished the commercial populations more rationally[65]. Their first and pretty amazing conclusion was that, using data from 2004, the current annual world catch of something approaching 100 million tonnes is worth about 5 billion dollars *less* than the cost of taking it! The only way this particular conundrum can be solved is through the huge programme of subsidies that western taxpayers dole out to fishermen to bridge the gap.

---

63 And some excellent books on the subject. For example Callum Roberts' *The Unnatural History of the Sea*, published by Gaia in 2007, and Charles Clover's *The End of the Line*, published by Ebury Press in 2004 and subsequently made into a hard-hitting documentary film in 2009.

64 The Food and Agriculture Organization, an arm of the United Nations.

65 Ragnar Arnason, Kieran Kelleher and Rolf Willman, *The Sunken Billions: The Economic Justification for Fisheries Reform*. The World Bank, Washington DC and FAO Rome.

49 Why are there so many Chinese fishing boats around the world?

It seems that no matter what major port you go into, almost anywhere in the world, you will find at least one, and usually several, Chinese fishing vessels. The reason, according to Food and Agriculture Organisation (FAO) statistics, is that there are more Chinese fishing vessels and many, many more Chinese fishermen than there are of any other nation on earth. The figures have to be treated with some caution because FAO admit that the statistics are difficult to check and the information coming out of China is particularly questionable. Nevertheless, the basic conclusion, that China is now dominating the fishing scene, is undoubtedly correct. Accepting this caution, here are some interesting figures.

The data for 1998, the latest year for which statistics are available, suggest that out of a total world fleet of about 1.3 million decked fishing vessels, almost 500,000 were Chinese. Similarly, in 2000, out of an estimated total fisheries-related workforce (including aquaculture or fish farming) of 13.5 million, 12.2 million were Chinese.

These figures represent a huge change in the last 40 years. In the early 1970s there were less than 50,000 Chinese fishing vessels at a time when Japan dominated world fishing with some 400,000 vessels. After a meteoric rise in the late 1970s, the Chinese fleet overtook Japan's, which has subsequently fallen to some 300,000 vessels. And while these dramatic changes in the fleets were taking place, the Chinese fisheries workforce increased from 2.3 to 12.2 million, while Japan's fell from 550,000 to only 250,000.

During this same period, China almost inevitably became the world's biggest producer of fish and fisheries projects. In 2000, China's total landings from both marine and inshore fisheries amounted to 17 million tonnes out of a world total of 95 million tonnes. In second place was Peru (largely based on the recovering anchoveta fishery), landing almost 11 million tonnes, followed by Japan (5 million), USA (4.7 million) and Chile (4.3 million). In 11th place (after Indonesia, the Russian Federation, India, Thailand and Norway) was Iceland, producing 2 million tonnes, while UK fishermen produced just over 700 thousand tonnes.

Finally, China is also by far the world's biggest consumer of fish. With her population having increased from about 800 million in 1970 to some 1,250 million in 2000, the net per capita annual consumption of fish, again according to the FAO, has apparently increased from 4.4kg (9.7lb) in 1972 to 25.1kg (55.3lb) in 1999. No wonder Chinese fishermen are everywhere!

50 How important is fish farming?

Fish farming, or more properly 'aquaculture', is a broad term referring to the cultivation of aquatic plants and animals, including fish and shellfish, in captivity as opposed to exploiting wild populations by fishing. The practice is hundreds, if not thousands, of years old. For example, the Romans cultivated mussels almost two thousand years ago, freshwater fish have been cultivated in Europe and Africa since medieval times, while fish and crustacean cultivation has a similarly long history in Asia. However, it is only in the last 50 years or so that intense fish and shellfish farming, employing fairly advanced technology, has become widespread.

According to FAO figures, in 1970 aquaculture accounted for just 3.9% of the total production from all fisheries resources, both freshwater and marine, but by the year 2000 this had grown to a massive 27.3%. In fact, as a source of world protein, aquaculture grew at an average rate of 9.2% each year between 1970 and 2000, compared with only 1.4% for capture fisheries and 2.8% for terrestrial meat production systems. In view of the dire situation in most conventional fisheries (see Q29, Q48), perhaps aquaculture will offer at least a partial solution to the problem of supplying protein to an increasingly populated world.

On the other hand, aquaculture in general, and intensive fish-farming in particular, has many opponents who see it as the source of a number of potential or actual problems. For instance, keeping lots of animals together in high densities carries a serious risk of encouraging the development of epidemic diseases, with the associated possibility of transmission to the wild populations. Similarly, passionate opponents of genetic modification (GM) see such practices – already being used to enhance the characteristics of farmed fish, such as growth rate and maximum size – as presenting a possible danger to wild populations if these 'bio-engineered monsters' should escape. Finally, and much more basically, the use of wild-caught fish and shellfish to feed the farmed stocks is seen as an encouragement for the over-exploitation of wild populations that are, in many cases, already under serious threat.

Despite these concerns, marine aquaculture seems to be firmly established. As a result, consumers in the west have become very familiar with farmed salmon from north-western Europe, tuna from the Mediterranean, tilapia from Africa, jumbo prawns from Indonesia and scallops from South America. But it will perhaps come as no surprise to learn that any growth in aquaculture in these, and most other regions has been totally dwarfed by the changes in China. Although FAO admits that their figures may be somewhat exaggerated, they suggest that between 1970 and 2000 China's freshwater and marine aquaculture production increased annually by an average of 11.5% and 14% respectively, both much higher than in the rest of the world. As a result, China's total aquaculture production in 2000 amounted to some 24 million tonnes out of a total world production of 35.6 million tonnes! Watch this space!

51 What is the Marine Stewardship Council?

The Marine Stewardship Council or MSC is an independent, non-profit-making organisation with the mission to 'reward sustainable fishing practices' by certificating wild fisheries that comply with its environmental standards. Products from these fisheries can then carry the MSC logo (see Fig 24) as a guide to potential consumers wishing to support environmentally sustainable activities.

The Council was originally founded in 1997 as an unlikely alliance between the World Wide Fund for Nature (WWF), the world's biggest environmental body, and Unilever Ltd, one of the world's largest fish buyers. Both organisations had independently come to the conclusion that many of the world's fish stocks were being seriously overfished and that the best way to tackle the problem was to inform the consuming public which stocks were being managed best so that they could choose which fish products to buy and which to avoid. Having established the system, in 1999 both WWF and Unilever stepped back and the MSC became a fully independent charity receiving funding from many different sources, with about half of its income coming, according to its website, from 'charitable grants'. It was originally based in London, where its headquarters still are. But the MSC now

Figure 24
The MSC logo (drawn rather badly by me). The white tick and fish outline should be against a bright blue background.

(mid-2010) has several offices around the world and employs about 60 personnel.

The MSC website, www.msc.org, says that more than 5,000 marine products worldwide currently carry its approval logo, the relevant fisheries organisation having successfully applied for MSC certification. The success or failure of an application is based on an independent assessment of the impact of the fishery on the target species and on the marine environment in general. After 10 years of independent existence, the MSC had certificated 42 fisheries around the world[66], ranging (alphabetically) from the Alaska salmon fishery to the Western Australian rock lobster fishery, with the complete list being available on the website.

The list includes some pretty big fisheries like the Alaskan salmon fishery (landing almost 300,000 tonnes a year), the Patagonian scallop fishery (landing about 45,000 tonnes a year) and the North Sea pelagic trawl herring fishery, with an annual catch of around 65,000 tonnes. But it also includes some much smaller, almost artisanal, fisheries, like the hand-raking cockle fishery in Burry inlet, South Wales, which produces less than 1,000 tonnes a year, and the 24 small boats in the Hastings fleet fishing for Dover sole, herring and mackerel.

I strongly support the MSC and its objectives and would advise anyone concerned about the marine environment to buy seafood carrying the MSC logo wherever possible, even though they currently cover only a very tiny percentage of world fisheries and very few indeed in the developing world. Nevertheless, like all such organisations, it needs to review its methods and decisions continuously to ensure its standards are maintained. By no means all of its certifications have gone uncriticised by conservation groups. For example, its certification of the Pacific pollack fishery and some Pacific salmon fishing has been questioned, as well as its 'approval' of the New Zealand hoki fishery (see Q33). For most of the fisheries involved I am unqualified to make a decision one way or the other so, like most people, I tend to give MSC the benefit of the doubt until someone or other convinces me otherwise. However, there is just one tiny area in which I have a modicum of experience – the fisheries for scampi, *Nephrops norvegicus* (see Q52 and Fig 25).

52 How sustainable are trawl fisheries?

In *Do Whales...?*, I explained that scampi, known in English as the Dublin Bay prawn or, more properly, the Norway lobster, is, indeed, a close relative of the familiar blue lobster of the fishmonger's slab, but in this case is reddish-orange in life, whereas the true lobster turns red only when it is cooked. *Nephrops* live

---

66   As I write this in July 2010, the MSC website says that 89 fisheries are now certificated.

Figure 25
Scampi on the hoof. A Norway lobster photographed in its natural habitat at the entrance to its burrow in a muddy Scottish sea floor. Photo courtesy of Nick Bailey, Fisheries Laboratory, Aberdeen.

in burrows on soft muddy seabed and generally only come out to feed and to mate. They live down to depths of 700–800m (2,300–2,625ft) but they can also be found in much shallower depths, as long as the bottom is suitable. And there are lots of suitable areas around the British, and particularly Scottish coasts, where they are the subject of extremely important fisheries.

One of the first British fisheries certificated by the MSC was the *Nephrops* creel fishery in Loch Torridon on the north-western coast of Scotland, an area I know quite well. My interest dates back to the late 1960s when Colin Chapman, a scientist pal from the Scottish fisheries laboratory in Aberdeen, invited me to join him and his team in a study of the Upper Loch Torridon *Nephrops* population. At the time, Colin was working on fish hearing and needed a quiet sea area to conduct his experiments. Upper Loch Torridon fitted the bill admirably, and when Colin's team started to install their equipment they found that the floor of the loch was populated by a wonderful community of Norway lobsters, excavating their burrows in the bottom mud at depths as shallow as 30m (about 100ft); this provided an excellent opportunity to study their biology – and a pretty nice place to do it in. As a result, for several years Colin's family and mine spent about a month each summer in the Torridon area, the wives looking after the kids (and us) and the men having a whale of a time diving on the *Nephrops* grounds. At the time, apart from us and a few salmon anglers, the peace of the loch was disturbed by only one creel fisherman fishing for prawns (as *Nephrops* are known in Scotland). Since those halcyon days the fishery has grown somewhat, though there are still only about 13 vessels engaged in it, most of them less than 10m (33ft) long and together taking only about 120 tonnes of *Nephrops* each year. Because they all use creels, the impact on the seabed is minimal and the fishermen can easily return undersized animals or females carrying eggs to the sea with every chance that they will suffer no long-term harm[67]. And the animals they keep will be in superb condition, having walked into the creel of their own volition in search of an easy meal. Sadly, the Torridon *Nephrops* are apparently almost exclusively exported to Spain, presumably because the Spanish are more willing to pay for this level of quality than we Brits are.

In April 2009 the Council certificated another Scottish *Nephrops* fishery, this time in the Minch, the body of water between the Outer Hebrides and mainland Scotland, and based in Stornoway on the Isle of Lewis. In contrast to the tiny Loch Torridon landings, although the Stornoway fishery has only 20-odd boats it has an annual catch of some 17,000 tonnes; clearly, it is much less labour intensive and its catches must be much cheaper. Not surprisingly, then, most of it apparently goes to Young's Seafoods[68], the huge Grimsby-based seafood processor and distributor, partly for the southern European frozen market and partly for the UK scampi tail market.

So how can this be? Well, it is simply because, instead of baited traps or creels, the fishery employs otter trawls – that is, large conical nets that are dragged across the seabed with the mouth held open by flat panels (otter boards), angled in such a way that they act a bit like underwater kites. Compared with beam trawls which, as the name suggests, have a net attached to a heavy wooden or metal beam to keep them open and firmly on the bottom, otter trawls cause much less physical damage to the sea floor. Nevertheless, all trawls leave a swathe of destruction behind them, and they don't distinguish the target species from other beasts living in the same area. Consequently, trawls always bring up a whole raft of stuff – the so-called by-catch – that the fisherman doesn't want and usually throws back into the sea. Having been scraped off the bottom, mixed together with mud, sand, stones and goodness knows what in the back end of

---

67   In fact, rather few egg-bearing females are taken in creels. This is because, once they have laid their eggs (carried glued to the underside of the tail), females stop feeding and stay mostly in the burrow until it is time to hatch the eggs in the spring. So only males and un-egged females are usually attracted to the baited traps.

68   To its credit, this more than 200-year-old company is at least trying to project an environmentally responsible image through its 'Fish for Life' programme, under which it claims that it deals only with fisheries and fish-farming organisations that comply with its 'Ten principles for responsible fish procurement', published on its website.

the net, most of the by-catch, including undersized members of the target species, is usually in pretty poor condition and unlikely to survive.

In its blurb on the Stornoway fishery, the MSC points out that the Minch population of *Nephrops* seems to be in good shape and quite capable of sustaining itself against the depredations of the fishery, and that the nets are fished on the bottom for relatively short periods in order to minimise the physical damage. Moreover, they say, the nets are fitted with some sort of 'lifting bag' to prevent it from coming into contact with the sea floor. I assume this means a system for lifting the 'cod' end – that is, the end bit of the net where the catch accumulates. Since *Nephrops* adults live entirely on or in the bottom mud, a net that did not make contact with the bottom would be pretty ineffective. Anyway, taking all of this into consideration, and having a rough idea of how much sea floor would have to be scraped to collect 17,000 tonnes of *Nephrops,* I have a niggling doubt about just how sustainable and therefore certifiable such a fishery is. And if the Stornoway *Nephrops* fishery trawls a lot of seabed, how much of the Continental Shelf of South America does the Patagonian scallop fishery (see Q19), also based on otter trawls, have to sweep to bring up 45,000 tonnes of them each year!

In truth, I have no idea whether these, and lots of other certificated trawl fisheries around the world, are really sustainable and don't do too much damage to the rest of the marine environment. So I have to take MSC's experts' word for it. What I do know is that bottom trawls generally are extremely damaging to the seabed and their effects can be seen for years after they have been used – so my view is that in an ideal world trawls wouldn't be used. Instead, we would all eat line-caught cod, creel-caught lobsters and diver-collected scallops. But I realise that this is an unrealistic objective, because few of us are willing to pay enough for seafood to justify these very labour intensive techniques. So trawls and other less-than-ideal fishing techniques are likely to be with us for the foreseeable future.

In the meantime, what can the environmentally concerned potential seafood purchaser do? Well, I suggest any number of possibilities. First, and best, look for the MSC logo. Despite the criticisms levelled at this system, at the moment it seems to be the best guarantee that you are buying something from a responsible supplier. At the very least it indicates that the fishery itself was sufficiently concerned about its image to apply to the MSC for certification, which suggests that their hearts are in the right place. If the MSC logo is not there, read the packaging and see if the supplier/producer makes any reference at all to sustainability, such as, for instance, the Young's Seafood Fish for Life program. Such a reference might, of course, simply be a bit of PR flannel, but at least, like with the MSC certification, it suggests that someone in the supply chain has given it some thought. Finally, ask the person behind the fish counter – whether it is in a supermarket or a traditional fishmonger – where their fish and shellfish come from and whether

the sources are sustainable. If you are greeted by a blank stare or a load of unconvincing gobbledegook, walk away and tell them that you won't come back until
they get their act together.

53 What are Marine Protected Areas?

Marine Protected Areas (MPAs) are defined by the International Union for the
Conservation of Nature (IUCN), an arm of the United Nations, as 'any area of the
intertidal or subtidal terrain, together with its overlying water and associated flora,
fauna, historical and cultural features, which has been reserved by law or other
effective means to protect part or all of the enclosed environment'. The term is
therefore a very general one that includes a wide variety of maritime situations,
ranging from areas within which all human activities are totally prohibited to
those in which only one activity – for example, commercial fishing or mineral
extraction – are banned, while all other activities are still allowed.

The history of fishing restrictions in certain areas of the sea to try to prevent
overfishing goes back hundreds of years, but the modern phase dates only from
the 1970s, when fishing restrictions were applied to a number of small areas in
the Pacific Ocean. Since that time, marine reserves of various types have mush-
roomed, not only for the conservation of exploitable species, but also for more
general conservation of marine biodiversity, particularly following the United
Nations 'biodiversity' summit in Rio de Janeiro in 1992.

There are now many hundreds of MPAs around the world, ranging from tiny
areas just a few kilometres square to huge reserves like the 340,000 km^2 (131,275
square mile) Great Barrier Reef Marine Park, established as early as 1975 by the
Queensland and Australian National Governments. Most MPAs are located fairly
close inshore, mainly within territorial waters and the contiguous zone (that is
within 24 nautical miles of the coastline) since these areas are relatively easy to
police by the neighbouring coastal state. However, in recent years there has been
a growing concern among marine scientists and conservationists that such protection should be extended to some offshore areas including the high seas, outside
the jurisdiction of individual nations. In the Mediterranean, for example, the
governments of France, Monaco and Italy established the Pelagos Sanctuary for
Mediterranean Marine Mammals in the Ligurian Sea, including not only portions
of each country's Exclusive Economic Zone but also high seas waters. Similarly,
the Darwin Mounds, an area of some 100km^2 (40 square miles) at a depth of
some 1,000m (3,280ft), about 180km (112 miles) north-west of Cape Wrath in
Scotland, has been given permanent protection from bottom trawling by the

EEC because they harbour important cold-water coral reefs (see Q6).

It is likely that, over the next few years, other important deep-water habitats, such as hydrothermal vents, will also be afforded MPA status by international agreement.

54 Who controls whaling?

The only body with any significant authority to control whaling is an organisation called the International Whaling Commission (IWC), with its headquarters at Impington near Cambridge, England. But as we are made only too well aware by the regular news reports of clashes between whaling vessels, particularly Japanese ones, and various environmental pressure groups, the Commission's powers are strictly limited. But in order to understand the working of the Commission today, we need to look back at its origin more than 60 years ago.

Prior to the Second World War, control of whaling was virtually non-existent. For the previous several hundreds of years, whaling ships had wandered the world's oceans, slaughtering whales and dolphins more or less indiscriminately. In the days of sailing ships and harpoons thrown by hand from rowing boats, the numbers taken had relatively little effect on the total populations. But with the development in the 1860s of the murderous explosive grenade harpoon, fired from the bows of fast steam-powered whale catchers, the situation changed dramatically. Not only did the new technology allow much greater numbers of the traditionally exploited whale species to be taken, but it also made the much faster-swimming rorquals vulnerable to hunting for the first time[69]. As a result, by the end of the 19th century the traditionally exploited whale stocks in the tropics and in the northern parts of the Atlantic and Pacific Oceans had become so seriously depleted that in many areas their exploitation was no longer economically viable. The situation was temporarily 'saved' by the opening up of the previously unexploited Antarctic whaling grounds at the beginning of the 20th century[70] and the development of pelagic whaling in the 1920s, in which the whale carcasses were processed at sea in factory ships instead of having to be taken ashore to land-based processing plants.

Although signs of overfishing of the Antarctic whale populations became

69 The rorquals are the 'big six' whalebone whales ranging from the minke whale at about 10m (33ft) long to the huge blue whale at more than 30m (100ft) long (see Do Whales...? Q74).

70 The first Antarctic whale taken commercially was caught on 27 November 2001 (see Rosalind Marsden, 2005, Discovery Investigations: An early attempt at ecologically sustainable development?, Archives of Natural History 32 (2): pp161–176).

apparent within a few years, the whaling companies[71] continued to expand their activities and slaughtered more and more whales. As a result, by the late 1920s and early 1930s there was a temporary over-production of whale oil and the whaling industry's own early attempt to regulate the catches was based on maintaining the oil price rather than protecting the whale populations. The main whaling companies agreed between themselves to limit production with restrictions on catches and particularly on the amount of oil produced; however, this arrangement failed when first Japan and then Germany began serious whaling in the mid-1930s but failed to comply with the proposed limits.

In the meantime, in 1931 the League of Nations[72] had attempted to establish a grand-sounding International Agreement for the Regulation of Whaling – again, like the failed voluntary agreement, mainly for maximising efficiency rather than for conserving the whales. This agreement didn't come into effect until 1937, mostly because Britain, one of the main whaling nations, was slow to ratify it. Even then, it was a pretty toothless piece of legislation because neither Japan nor Germany would agree to it. Moreover, one of the agreement's well intentioned but disastrous consequences was the introduction of the concept of the Blue Whale Unit (BWU).

The idea was intended to provide a way of comparing different whale species for the purposes of quotas and limits, this comparison being based on the presumed amount of oil that a typical or average specimen of each species would provide. So while a blue whale represented, not surprisingly, one BWU, a fin whale was assumed to produce only half as much oil so that two fin whales would equal one BWU. Similarly, two and a half humpback whales or six sei whales would be equivalent to one BWU, while other exploited species were assigned other conversion factors. From a purely industrial point of view the BWU system was fine for setting up limits on the total numbers of whales that could be caught in a given year. But for whale conservation it was disastrous. Whalers inevitably concentrated on the very largest specimens and may even have discarded smaller specimens in favour of larger ones when approaching the limits of the quota[73].

---

71   Mostly British and Norwegian in the early years of the century, until the Japanese and Germans entered the fray in the 1930s.
72   The League of Nations was established in 1920 as a sort of international peace club to try to resolve international conflict and prevent a repetition of the disastrous events surrounding the First World War. Apart from its primary role of intervening in typical political controversies, the League also addressed other issues as diverse as health, the rights of women, slavery – and whaling. Having failed to prevent the Second World War, the League of Nations was replaced by the United Nations in 1946.
73   The same thing happens today in some strictly controlled fisheries in which fishermen are reported to fill their holds up to their quota limit, but to continue fishing in order to replace smaller fish with more valuable larger ones, the replaced ones simply being thrown back into the sea.

In the last few years before the Second World War, a number of useful conservation measures were introduced through the League of Nations. These included establishing minimum sizes of each species that could be taken, restrictions on killing female whales accompanied by calves, total protection for some species including the right whales and Pacific gray whales, and a total ban on taking humpbacks. In any case, the whale populations were given a bit of a respite because whaling virtually ceased for the duration of the war. But with its resumption after the ending of hostilities, first by Norway and Britain but soon followed by the Soviet Union, Japan, South Africa and Holland, it was obvious that further regulations would be needed. So when the League of Nations was replaced by the United Nations in 1946, the old Regulation of Whaling duties were transferred to the newly established International Whaling Commission.

The new Commission adopted the restrictions that had been put in place before the war, but with a remit to 'provide for the proper conservation of whale stocks and thus make possible the orderly development of the whaling industry', its loyalties were clearly seen to be towards the industry rather than to the whales. Consequently, at its first meeting in 1949 the IWC removed the ban on taking humpbacks and allowed a quota of 1,250 – which was largely ignored anyway! At the same time the Commission introduced a quota of 16,000 BWU for the Antarctic whale fishery, resulting in no less than 32,566 whales being taken by the 20 factory ships operating during the 1950–51 season. Subsequent attempts to restrict the annual whale catch met with no more success and signs of serious depletion of the stocks became apparent. Despite the best, or worst, efforts of the whaling companies to catch them, blue whale captures crashed in the late 1950s, followed by those of fin whales and sei whales in the 1960s. By the 1970s the whaling companies were having to transfer their efforts to the smallest of the rorquals, the minke whale. Whaling was becoming less and less economically viable and, during the 1960s, Britain, Holland and Norway all pulled out of the Antarctic, leaving only Japan and the Soviet Union still exploiting the Southern Ocean whales.

Also during the early 1970s, as a result of the activities of protest groups such as Greenpeace and Sea Shepherd (see Q55), there was a growing public awareness of the appalling cruelty of the whaling industry. The increasing global opposition to whaling began to have an impact on the IWC as more and more non-whaling or anti-whaling nations began to join it. Nevertheless, it was still dominated by whaling nations so that when, in 1972, the United Nations Conference on the Human Environment called for a ten-year moratorium on whaling, it was rejected by the IWC with a majority of six to four against, with four member nations abstaining. But things were about to change!

Although there had never been any restriction on membership of the Whaling Commission, in its early days only those with a more or less direct commercial interest in whaling seemed anxious to join it. Consequently, the initial members were only Australia, France, Norway, the Soviet Union, South Africa, the UK and the USA, shortly to be joined by Mexico, Denmark and Japan. Argentina joined in 1960 and there was a further trickle of new members over the next 30 to 40 years. But this trickle has turned into something of a torrent in recent years, so that since 2001 membership of the IWC has more than doubled and in 2010 it stands at 88 nations – most of them bitterly opposed to whaling. By 1982 the balance of pro- and anti-whaling members had changed so much that the IWC annual meeting adopted a recommendation for a total moratorium on commercial whaling to come into effect in 1986, despite the objections of the Soviet Union, Japan and Norway.

Many onlookers thought, and hoped, that this would finally mark an end to whaling – but it didn't. First, since its inception the International Whaling Commission had always recognised that so-called aboriginal subsistence whaling (see Q55) should be treated differently from commercial whaling. But in any case, the IWC has no statutory control over whaling and any restrictions it imposes are essentially voluntary. So any member nation that disagrees with an IWC proposed restriction can simply lodge an objection within 90 days and then set its own rules – amazing! And if it doesn't fancy this route, any member state can claim that it needs to catch whales for scientific purposes and apply to the IWC for a so-called special permit to catch a specified number of various whale species. Both ploys have been used, particularly by Norway and Japan, Norway concentrating on the objection route and Japan on the fatuous scientific argument. Consequently, according to the IWC's own published figures, since the supposedly total moratorium on commercial whaling came into force in 1986, up to the 2008/2009 season (the last for which figures are available), no less than 20,248 whales have been slaughtered under the 'objection' rule and 13,313 under the 'scientific permit' one[74]. The whales would surely be greatly relieved to know how well their interests are being looked after by the International Whaling Commission! This is admittedly a slightly unfair comment, since the Commission can do only what its rules and its members allow it to.

Nevertheless, many onlookers hope and expect the organisation to take a rather more robust anti-whaling stance than it generally seems to. Perhaps it will under its new Secretary, Dr Simon Brockington, Head of Conservation for the Marine Conservation Society (see Q56), who took over the IWC position at the annual

---

74   Broken down by species, these numbers are made up of 30,971 minke whales, 1,180 Bryde's whales, 662 sei whales, 435 sperm whales and 313 fin whales, for a shameful grand total of 33,561!

meeting in Agadir, Morocco. As I write this section, in June 2010, the annual meeting is receiving its customary fairly lurid coverage in the world's press. This time the meeting will be considering a proposal put forward by the out-going chairman that the 24-year-old moratorium should be replaced by a new agreement in which the IWC would have greater powers in regulating whaling in return for allowing a relatively low level of commercial whaling. The pro-whaling nations – Greenland, Norway and Japan – would clearly favour such a move[75]. But the proposal has split the anti-whaling lobby, some, such as the Whale and Dolphin Conservation Society, being totally opposed to any suggestion of recognising commercial whaling at any level, while others, including Greenpeace, believe that such a move might offer the best chance of conserving whale populations in the long term. Watch this space.

55 What is aboriginal subsistence whaling?

Aboriginal subsistence whaling is the exploitation of whales in relatively small numbers by groups of indigenous peoples, often with a long traditional history, to satisfy cultural and material needs in local communities. The International Whaling Commission (see Q54) recognises such subsistence whaling as quite different from so-called 'commercial' whaling and adopts a quite different attitude towards it.

Accordingly, the current IWC regulations allow subsistence whaling by local peoples for fin and minke whales around Greenland, for gray and bowhead whales off Siberia and Alaska, and for humpback whales off Bequia in the Caribbean.

A number of other local whale fisheries occur around the world but are not overseen by the IWC. In the North Atlantic, sperm whales had been hunted around the Azores and Madeira since the practice of hand-harpooning from rowing boats was introduced to the locals by American whalers in the early 19th century. The Azoreans, in particular, continued the practice into the late 20th century, still using open boats and hand-held harpoons but using engines to power the boats

---

75 Some of the most sensational news coverage has involved accusations that the Japanese have been trying to 'buy' the votes of some of the poorer member nations of the IWC by offers of financial aid and even providing the services of prostitutes to delegates visiting Japan. True or not, we all know that a whiff of sex is sure to attract otherwise uninterested journalists. To add just a little more zest to this already fairly potent mix, in the same week Sea Shepherd's founder and leader Captain Paul Watson was quoted as saying: 'We [Sea Shepherd] are rejecting the International Whaling Commission as a corrupt and irrelevant body that has lost all credibility as an organisation responsible for the conservation of the world's whales...'

to and from the whaling grounds. However, by the 1980s both sets of islands had abandoned whaling, attracting a much greater income from whale-watching tourists.

Unfortunately, the same is not true of what is possibly the most controversial of these fisheries, the annual Faroese hunt, mainly for long-finned pilot whales, *Globicephala melas,* but also for several dolphin species. Mainly pursued during the summer months, this fishery is hundreds of years old and is still considered an important part of Faroese culture. Traditionally, the hunt, called a *grindadráp,* is carried out from small boats that attempt to surround a pod of whales and drive them ashore, where they are slaughtered. Until the 1980s the hunters were allowed to use spears and harpoons to drive and disable the whales, along with a sharp hook or gaff to pull the still-living animals ashore to be finally dispatched. Since the early 1990s, however, these tools have been banned in favour of a blunt gaff used to pull the whale in by the blowhole and a special whaling knife used to kill it relatively quickly by severing the spinal cord. Annual catches in recent years have averaged a little under 1,000 animals which, although the subject of some considerable controversy, is probably sustainable in the sense that it is not significantly impacting the target species' population numbers. However, the widespread abhorrence of whale killing in general, coupled with the shockingly vivid images resulting from the large amount of blood entering the sea during the kill, makes the fishery a favourite target of conservation groups.

Less well known, and therefore attracting much less adverse attention, are a number of other subsistence whale fisheries pursued in various parts of the Indian Ocean and the Pacific. These include a sperm-whale fishery undertaken by natives of Lamalera, Indonesia, using long hand-held harpoons thrown from primitive rowing boats, and an even more remarkable hunt practised from the tiny island of Pamalican in the Philippines. Here, again from a rickety wooden sailing-cum-rowing boat, an incredibly athletic – and courageous – 'hook jumper' will leap into the sea to slam home a large steel hook on the end of a long rope through the tough skin of a manta ray, whale shark or even a 20-tonne Bryde's whale and hopefully regain the relative safety of the boat before the victim drags him off at an alarming and bone-crunching rate. Both fisheries are graphically described by explorer and adventurer Tim Severin in his excellent book *In Search of Moby Dick,* published by Little, Brown and Company in 1999.

56 What is the Marine Conservation Society?

The Marine Conservation Society is a UK charity for the protection, conservation and rational use of British shores and maritime waters and their wildlife.

It operates by education, lobbying and sponsoring specific projects. For instance, it runs a series of campaigns for clean beaches including an anti-litter campaign, an annual Beachwatch project in which volunteers clean specific beach areas and report the results, and it publishes an annual Good Beach Guide listing the best, and worst, of Britain's beaches.

The MCS is also closely involved in championing sustainable exploitation of marine resources by publishing information on which fisheries and species are considered to be operated sustainably, and by regularly surveying supermarket shelves and reporting on how they are performing against the MCS's sustainability criteria. They also work with the Marine Stewardship Council (confusingly abbreviated to the MSC as opposed to the MCS! – see Q51) to provide logo stickers for retailers to mark produce endorsed by the organisations.

Although the MCS is primarily a UK organisation, it is involved in research and conservation projects in many parts of the world, including marine turtles in the Caribbean and corals in Malaysia and the Indian Ocean.

Like the Whale and Dolphin Conservation Society, the MCS is considered pretty 'kosher' by politicians and celebs.

The MCS website is www.mcsuk.org.

57 What is the Whale and Dolphin Conservation Society?

The Whale and Dolphin Conservation Society (WDCS) is a non-governmental charitable organisation devoted solely to the conservation and welfare of whales, dolphins and porpoises worldwide. It was founded in 1987 and is based in the UK but has offices in Argentina, Australia, Austria, Germany and the USA.

The WDCS does not get involved in direct confrontation with the whaling industry. Instead, it attempts to achieve its objectives by a combination of lobbying, education and supporting active conservation projects and research into particularly vulnerable populations. It also encourages whale watching and endorses the eco-tourism company 'Out of the Blue'.

Because of its relatively non-controversial approach, the WDCS tends to attract the support of politicians, celebrities and other international organisations. For example, it is a partner in the United Nations Environment Programme Convention on Migratory Species. As its name suggests, this convention seeks to achieve international cooperation in the protection of terrestrial, avian and marine species whose migratory patterns cause them to cross national boundaries. Whales and dolphins are, of course, particularly important members of this group of species because they often spend much of their time in parts of the oceans that are not under the control of any individual nation (see *Do Whales...?* Q118).

The WDCS website is www.whales.org.

V

Ships and Sailors

As with the section on 'Ocean Facts and Figures', I tackled quite a few questions under the heading 'Ships and Sailors' in *Do Whales...?*, ranging from simple ones like the definition of a fathom or a nautical mile to more testing ones like the workings of a gyrocompass and how to calculate how far you can see from the deck of a ship. This time I've dealt with a similarly fairly eclectic group of questions, ranging from pretty mundane ones like why sailors spend so much time painting, to rather more esoteric ones like the workings of stabilisers and the nature of great circle routes. I hope you find both ends of the spectrum interesting

58 What is a great circle route?

A great circle route is one, would you believe, that follows a great circle. So what is a great circle? It is any line on the surface of the earth marking its circumference and with its centre coinciding with that of the earth. This sounds a bit complicated, but it isn't. Think of a great circle as analogous to the cut edge of slice through an apple made in any direction *as long as it passes through the apple's centre.*

All great circles divide the earth into two halves, so the most familiar great circle of all is the equator, dividing the earth into the northern and southern hemispheres. The equator is also, of course, a line of latitude, by convention labelled 0°. It is, however, the only line of latitude that is also a great circle. All other lines of latitude are smaller than the equator and their centres do not coincide with the centre of the earth. So they are not great circles.

On the other hand, all lines of longitude *are* great circles, or rather parts of great circles. Take, for example, the prime meridian – that is, longitude 0° (zero degrees), passing through Greenwich in south-east London. If you followed this line of longitude north it would eventually reach the geographic North Pole where it would meet its opposite number, longitude 180°, on the other side of the earth. Follow longitude 180° south and you would eventually come to the geographic South Pole and meet longitude 0° again. Following this line north, you would eventually get back to Greenwich and complete the circle centred on the earth's own centre and, just as in the case of the equator, you would have travelled a line that divides the earth into two equal hemispheres, this time the western and the eastern hemispheres. And you could do exactly the same with every other pair of complementary longitudes: for example 10°E and 170°W; 20°E and 160°W; 30°E and 150°W; 90°E and 90°W – and so on. So if you move due geographic north or south from any point on the earth's surface, or due east or west from any point on the equator, you will be travelling along a great circle route.

So what about lines over the earth's surface in other directions? Well, as long as they are on the circumference of a circle centred on the earth's centre, they too will be great circles or parts of great circles. You can visualise such routes quite easily by imagining (or actually!) sticking pins into two different positions on the surface of a model globe of the earth and joining them together with a piece of cotton. If you now pull the cotton as tightly as possible between the two pins it will be in contact with the surface of the globe along a part of a great circle and illustrates the fact that a great circle route is the shortest possible distance between any two points on the earth's surface. This is why planes flying from western Europe to west-coast destinations in the USA (Los Angeles, for example) tend to fly north over the pole rather than south-west, although this might seem a more rational direction from a perusal of a world map. But herein lies the rub.

A south-west course, and all other courses on compass bearings other than north, south, east and west, follow lines across the earth's surface called 'rhumb lines', defined as lines crossing all lines of longitude at the same angle. With a decent compass and reasonable weather, such a line is the easiest for a navigator to follow. But if you try to plot such a line on a globe you will notice that instead of being a reasonably straight line, it inexorably curves. Although it consistently crosses lines of longitude at the same angle, because these lines all converge at the poles, a rhumb line inevitably describes a spiral path around the globe, eventually reaching one or other of the poles. This was a huge problem for early navigators using maps that were trying to depict a spherical surface in two dimensions. With curved lines of longitude it was nigh on impossible to determine the course to steer between any two distant points. The Flemish cartographer Gerard Mercator (1512–94) solved the problem when he artificially straightened out lines of longitude and changed the spacing of lines of latitude so that, for the first time, rhumb lines on his maps were straight and showed the compass bearing between any two points on the earth's surface. The unfortunate downside was that the further you moved away from the equator, the more distorted shapes and distances are on Mercator's projection, so that it is fairly useless beyond latitudes of about 70° north and south.

However, even where a Mercator projection is usable, convenient though a single compass direction is to follow, a rhumb line cannot represent the shortest distance between two points on the earth's surface. Over short distances the effect is very small, but over thousands of miles this is the preserve of great circle routes. But to follow such a route accurately you have to change your compass heading continuously, which is a real pain. So ships and aircraft using great circle routes generally follow straight-line courses between a series of 'way points' that approximate the great circle but don't follow it faithfully.

On long-haul aircraft, most of us are too exhausted, bored or otherwise preoccupied to notice which specific route we are following and, in any case, planes flying over land are constrained by air traffic regulations. But at sea, things happen much more slowly and passengers can, and do, frequently take more interest in the ship's course. Most conventional cruises involve relatively short legs of no more than a couple of days between port calls, so that great circle routes are pretty irrelevant. Not so with long ocean crossings, where great circle routes can represent a considerable saving in both time and fuel, and can confuse the passengers!

Take, for example, the classic Southampton to New York passage, so famous in the heydays of the great ocean liners and now being reintroduced by Cunard as a civilised alternative to flying. Southampton is at a latitude of roughly 51°N and longitude 1°W. New York is at roughly 41°N and 74°W. This puts New York some 600 nautical miles south of Southampton and about 3,000 miles west. If you plot this out on a flat piece of paper, a compass bearing between the two would seem to be about 258° (technically known as west by south). But if you took the great circle route between Southampton and New York, your initial heading would be 287°, that is almost west-northwest, and it would take you over the Bristol Channel and the southern tip of Ireland! Now the master of a Cunarder leaving Southampton for New York has a little matter of the English Channel to negotiate before he can think of a great circle route. However, once the ship is out of the established traffic lanes and has cleared the western approaches, passengers are often surprised to see that their ship is heading somewhat to the north of west. They will now be on a great circle apparently taking them, on a Mercator projection, along a curving line across the North Atlantic before turning south to pass the Grand Banks off Newfoundland then proceed more or less parallel with the North American east coast to the latitude of New York before turning west for the final approach, having shortened the potential passage by several tens of nautical miles.

59 Why is a ship's bridge called a bridge?

Because the earliest ones looked exactly like a bridge (see Fig 26).

In the days of sail, and even today in most sailing vessels, ships were steered from a position close to the stern, either with a tiller bar attached directly to the rudder or by a wheel moving the rudder via ropes or chains. From such a position the helmsman had a clear view of the sails and of the way ahead. But in the early steam-driven ships, with a huge paddle wheel on either side, the view from such a stern position was obstructed by the paddle boxes and often also by the funnel. The tops of the paddle boxes were usually linked by an elevated walkway or 'bridge' and this was found to be a much more convenient place for the wheel and the ship's compass.

When paddles were replaced by screws, the wheel and compass remained on the 'bridge', now a raised platform across the middle part of the ship, which became the control centre patrolled by the officer of the watch. Initially, the bridge was open to the elements with protection provided only by canvas screens, as can be seen in HMS *Warrior*, preserved in Portsmouth, and Brunel's SS *Great Britain* in

Figure 26
The bridge of Brunel's SS Great Britain photographed in Bristol from the port side looking aft.

Bristol (see Fig 26). Gradually, however, the bridge evolved into the totally enclosed area fully integrated into the ship's superstructure that is typical today, albeit sometimes still with open bridge-wings on either side. Finally, the bridge has tended to migrate either forwards, as in most passenger carrying ships, or backwards, as in most cargo ships, particularly bulk carriers and container ships. But wherever it is, it is still called the bridge, reminding us of its origins.

60 When *do* eight bells toll[76]?

Ship's bells have an almost mystical role. They are usually made of brass, are mounted prominently on the foredeck, carry the ship's name, and often become a highly prized memento after the ship has been broken up.

These days, ships have all sorts of communication aids so that ship's bells are largely redundant other than as symbols. Traditionally, however, the ship's bell had a much more practical role. First, it was used as a fog signal where no other audible signal was available. But much more regularly the ship's bell was used to indicate the passage of time to the ship's company when very few of them would have possessed their own timekeepers.

For hundreds of years, the working day on a ship has been divided into six 'watches', each of four hours, so that the work of the ship's company can be organised to allow each of them to have adequate rest. Traditionally, except on very small ships, and during particularly critical manoeuvres like docking, the captain does not stand a watch – that is, occupy the bridge and take responsibility for driving the ship. Instead, the more junior deck officers, usually at least three on cruise ships, each spend two periods each of four hours on the bridge during a 24-hour day. The First Watch is the four hours from 8pm (ie 2000) to midnight; the Middle Watch is from midnight to 0400, the Morning Watch is from 0400 to 0800, the Forenoon Watch from 0800 to midday, and the Afternoon Watch from midday to 1600. So what happens between 1600 and 2000?

Most ship's companies are organised into two or three teams, confusingly also called watches. But to ensure that they do not always work the same *time* watches day after day, which would probably be prejudicial to efficiency, the 4pm (ie 1600)

---

76 *When eight bells toll* was a 1971 film based on a novel by Alistair MacLean staring a very young Anthony Hopkins as a British secret agent investigating a ship hijacking operation based in Scotland. The climax of the film begins with the ramming of an underground dock by shark fishermen enlisted by Hopkin's character, Phillip Calvert. The ramming takes place at midnight, that is at the end of the first watch and indicated by the tolling of eight bells, hence the title.

to 8pm (ie 2000) watch is divided into two 2-hour 'Dog' watches, the First Dog from 1600 to 1800 and the Last Dog from 1800 to 2000. This ensures that each 24 hours there are an odd number of watches (that is, seven) so that the work schedule of each individual keeps changing.

Within each watch, the passage of time was traditionally marked by a strike on the bell for each half hour. So one bell represented half an hour, two bells an hour, three bells 1½ hours and so on, until the end of the watch was marked by eight bells.

This was fine for all of the watches from the First Watch (2000 to midnight), throughout the night and morning, to the Afternoon Watch from noon to 1600. But as we have seen, just to complicate matters the 1600 to 2000 watch was divided into two dog watches, each of two hours. So four bells struck at 1800 mark the end of the First Dog Watch and one bell struck at 1830 marks the first half hour of the Second Dog Watch. Perversely, the end of the Second Dog Watch is marked by eight bells, as if it were the end of a conventional 4-hour watch. Sailors are nothing if not unpredictable, and now you know, more or less, when eight bells toll!

61 Why do sailors always seem to be painting?

It is rare to be on any ship for more than a few hours without coming across sailors rubbing down the rail, chipping paint off various bits of metal or recoating them with paint or varnish using rollers on long sticks or a variety of strange-shaped brushes. In fact, while the vessel is at sea you will rarely see a sailor doing anything else. Of course, when the ship is in the process of coming alongside a quay, or casting off after a port call, almost all of the sailors, perhaps a dozen or more on the big vessel, are busy at either end dealing with the ropes and all the other paraphernalia associated with tying up, and then rigging up the gangways. And in cruise ships that are too big to come alongside a quay and have to transfer passengers between the ship and the shore in tenders, it is the sailors who launch and re-stow the boats, man them during their to-and-fro transits and supervise the safety of passengers during embarkation and disembarkation. During the port call itself the sailors will also man winches, cranes and so on if fresh supplies or equipment have to be taken on board, and will also be involved in any refuelling or replenishing water supplies. Even so, when you come back from your trip ashore, as likely as not you will find one or more sailors standing on the quay painting the huge expanse of the ship's side with a ridiculously small-looking roller.

So why do these well-trained sea-going professionals spend so much of their time as painters and decorators? Basically, for two reasons – one fairly obvious and one possibly not so obvious. The obvious reason is that keeping a good coat of paint or varnish on a ship's metalwork and woodwork is essential to maintain the condition of any vessel exposed to the corrosive attack of seawater. So somebody has to do chipping and sanding and repainting. And like the maintenance of any large structure, such as a bridge or a huge building, keeping a ship in good nick is a never-ending process. Once you've finished at one end it is time to start again at the other. So there is always plenty of work.

The less obvious reason is that if the sailors didn't do all the painting, what would they do? In the days of wooden sailing ships things were very different. Like today, the fabric of the ship, then mostly wood, rope and canvas, still had to be maintained against the ravages of the sea and the weather. But much of this work was highly skilled, and a sailing ship crew would include teams of carpenters, riggers and sailmakers whose specific job was to attend to the maintenance. Relatively unskilled tasks – like cleaning and painting – would have been done then, as now, by sailors. But these would have been the lowliest and least technically adept of the sailors, because most of their non-officer shipmates would have been totally occupied with the multifarious tasks of dealing with the propulsion system – that is, the sails and rigging. These tasks were arduous, skilled, frequently dangerous – and very labour intensive. So sailing ships had much bigger crews that their modern-day equivalents, with a big ship needing perhaps a hundred or more men simply to sail her[77]. Among such huge complements there would be plenty of men to undertake all the other 'non-propulsive' tasks like anchoring, tying up, boat-handling and stowing provisions and cargo. But once the sails were superseded by steam and later by oil, the ship's propulsion was in the hands of a quite different set of technologists. And many fewer, because the engine rooms of the biggest vessels could be manned adequately by a handful of engineer officers backed by a relatively modest team of stokers and other subsidiary staff.

Now, when a ship was at sea, the need for all the pulling on rope and canvas and clambering up and down masts every time the course or the weather changed completely disappeared – and so did most of the sailors. Under normal conditions at sea, the small number of surviving seamen had rather little to do. One or two seamen were fairly routinely needed on the bridge to act as lookouts and helmsmen,

---

77 Military vessels needed even bigger crews because, in addition to the traditional sailors manning the sails and rigging, they had to include specialist fighters to man the guns, form boarding parties and repel potential boarders. They also needed marines, both to act as seagoing soldiers and to protect the officers from the crew if this became necessary – as it not infrequently did. Consequently, Horatio Nelson's famous flagship, the 69m (227ft) long HMS *Victory*, had a total complement of no less than 850, while the USS *Constitution*, only marginally shorter at 63m (204ft), though with one less gun deck, had a complement of 450, including 55 marines and 30 boys.

while in bad visibility one or two other lookouts might be required. But apart from keeping things on deck reasonably tidy, and tying movable objects down in advance of bad weather, that was about it. So what better occupation to keep idle hands and bored minds out of mischief than the unlimited and mindless task of chipping and painting. And that is the way it's been ever since.

62 Why do ships need pilots?

Pilots are qualified navigators with particular knowledge of a specific area – for example, the approaches to a port, or the passage through a channel or along a river. They are usually licensed and authorised by a national supervising authority, which also specifies the conditions under which a pilot must be taken on board and the fees to be charged.

In many ports and navigable waterways the local regulations make it compulsory for ships over a certain size to use the services of a pilot. Failure to do so not only contravenes these regulations but, in the event of anything untoward happening in the absence of a pilot, the ship's commander would be held personally responsible.

Curiously, even with a pilot on board the captain remains responsible for the vessel's safety, though pilotage regulations require him to follow the pilot's instructions – even if they are wrong!

Masters of cross-channel ferries, and of similar vessels that habitually enter pilotage waters, are usually qualified as pilots so that they do not have to embark one on their passages.

In the days before the development of radio communication, pilot cutters would wait at points of entry into pilotage waters to place pilots on incoming vessels and disembark them from departing vessels. But nowadays pilots are usually ordered well in advance and are 'delivered' and 'disembarked' from client ships by powerful, fast, and usually very smart pilot launches or even, on occasion, by helicopters.

63 How do stabilisers work?

Stabilisers are fitted to most modern ships to try to reduce the vessels' tendency to roll – that is, to lean from one side to the other – in rough weather. Stabilisers can be either 'passive' – that is, requiring no energy input from the vessel – or 'active' and involving the use of pumps, pistons or some other control system.

The simplest form of passive stabiliser is the bilge keel, a strip of metal welded to the outside of the ship's hull and running almost the length of the vessel below the waterline, usually close to where the ship's side changes from more or less vertical to more horizontal. The idea is simply that the keel increases the resistance to the ship's tendency to roll.

A rather more sophisticated passive system is the use of anti-roll tanks, installed in many older vessels. These consist of a system of water-filled tanks situated low down in the ship's hull and fitted with baffles that slow down the passage of water from one side to the other as the vessel rolls. Here, the intention is to trap more water on the higher side and therefore help to dampen the roll and bring the vessel back to a vertical position.

Anti-roll tanks can also be active, in which case they are fitted with pumps and pipes used to transfer water rapidly from one side of the vessel to the other automatically in response to the ship's tendency to lean and to counteract it.

Many passenger vessels are fitted with active stabilising fins. These are wing-like structures, up to 6 or 7m long (20–23ft) on very large vessels, that protrude from the hull on either side. They are connected to a control and driving mechanism inside the hull, which rotates the fin in response to the ship's movement to alter its angle as it moves through the water. These fins therefore act just like the hinged flaps or ailerons on the trailing edges of aeroplane wings, which counteract the plane's tendency to roll. These active systems in ships are, of course, expensive, both in using energy to drive them and particularly by increasing the vessel's resistance in its passage through the water. Consequently, the most sophisticated versions are retractable inside the hull in fair weather when they are not required.

Finally, fins depend for their performance on a significant forward motion through the water. They are therefore of little use when a ship is hove to – that is more or less stationary – or moving forwards very slowly. For these situations, gyroscopic stabilisers have been developed in recent years to hold a vessel steady against any disturbing influence. Such systems have been used successfully in small vessels, including yachts, but have not been successfully applied to large ships.

64 What is the connection between Lloyd's Register, Lloyd's of London and Lloyds Bank?

Virtually nothing, apart from the word 'Lloyd'.

First let's deal with the bank. The name Lloyd in Lloyds Bank has absolutely no connection with the other two. It is derived from Sampson Lloyd, an iron producer in Birmingham, who set up a banking business with a button maker named John Taylor in 1765. In contrast, Lloyd's Register and Lloyd's of London got their names a century earlier from Edward Lloyd, who ran a coffee shop in the 1680s in Tower Street in London.

Now let's look at the other two linked by a coffee shop in 17th century London. Lloyd's coffee shop in Tower Street in the city of London was a popular meeting place for all sorts of businessmen, including merchants, shipowners and mariners. To encourage their patronage, the owner, Edward Lloyd, produced a regular news-sheet with all sorts of snippets about the shipping industry. This arrangement continued when the coffee shop moved to Lombard Street in 1691 and even after Edward Lloyd's death in 1713. The little news-sheet evolved into Lloyd's List (not to be confused with Lloyd's Register (see below)), now published daily and approaching its 60,000th edition. It is one of the oldest continuously published journals in the world and includes information on all aspects of maritime activities including, most famously, all marine mishaps.

In the meantime, in 1774, a number of the participants in the maritime insurance activities moved from the Lombard Street coffee house to the Royal Exchange as 'The Society of Lloyd's'. Their association was basically to pool and spread insurance risks – and it still is. Initially, the business was entirely maritime and, for a long time, principally associated with the slave trade. But gradually the range of interests increased until, today, Lloyd's of London members will insure virtually anything.

Back in the early days, when the insurance business was still being enacted in Lloyd's coffee house, the merchants and underwriters needed to know the condition of the vessels they were chartering or insuring. In 1760, a number of the coffee shop customers got together to form the Lloyd's Register Society, a not-for-profit maritime classification organisation to provide this information. It produced its first *Register of Ships* in 1764, using an alphanumeric system for grading ships – letters for the condition of the hull and numbers for the ship's fittings. Thus, the top rating became A1, giving rise to the expression 'A1' or 'A1 at Lloyd's' to indicate anything that is considered to be of top quality.

65 Who are Maersk?

All over the world you see ships, particularly container ships, with the word 'Maersk' painted on the side in huge letters (see Fig 27). And even if a container ship isn't a Maersk one, a high proportion of any containers it may be carrying are almost certain to be Maersk's. So who are Maersk?

Maersk is part of a huge organisation, the AP Moller-Maersk Group, with its head office in Copenhagen, Denmark, and with offices in around 130 countries. It was originally founded in 1904 by Arnold Peter Moller and his father Captain Peter Maersk Moller (which is where the 'Maersk' bit comes from). The firm started with the purchase of a second-hand 2,200 tonne steamer, but in the intervening century has expanded to employ about 120,000 people worldwide, engaged in a vast range of activities including the energy (oil and gas) industry, shipbuilding and manufacturing. Among its many activities, Maersk is a world leader in the container shipping industry, owning some 220 of its own vessels and operating an additional 300 or so. In 1999 the Moller-Maersk group acquired Sea-Land Service, a company operating some 70 container ships and about 200,000 containers.

As at April 2009, the Maersk Line and Safmarine fleet of container vessels consisted of about 500 vessels and about a million containers corresponding to almost 2 million TEUs[78]. These ships range in capacity from about 650 TEUs (*Maersk Erimo*) to 11,000 TEUs (several vessels with girl's names followed by Maersk, for example *Eleonora Maersk, Estelle Maersk* and *Emma Maersk*). Maersk also operates crude oil and liquefied gas carriers, car and truck transporters and a number of RO/RO and RO/PAX, the latter under the name Norfolkline, as well as less special-ised vessels for the transport of many other products. Finally, other subsidiaries – Maersk Contractors and Maersk Supply Service – operate a variety of drilling rigs and more than 40 oil and gas industry servicing vessels.

66 What are container ships?

Container ships, informally known as 'box boats', are cargo ships that carry their load in truck-sized containers piled in huge stacks. The first purpose-built container ships were constructed in the 1950s and rapidly became popular with shipping companies because of the ease of handling the cargo in standard containers. Today, about 90% of all non-bulk cargo is carried in container ships and they have become one of the commonest sights in many parts of the ocean.

Capacity of container ships is measured in TEUs (twenty-foot equivalent) units based on standard containers measuring 20 x 8 x 8.5ft (6.1 x 2.4 x 2.6m), though most containers used today are twice this size (40ft/12m long).

The ships come in a range of sizes, with the largest plying deep-sea routes between major container-handling ports like Rotterdam and Felixstowe, and smaller vessels

---

78   Twenty-foot equivalent units (ie containers), see Q66.

serving smaller ports. The largest container ships currently have capacities of some 15,000 TEUs but even larger vessels are planned. In 2008 the South Korean Shipbuilder STX announced plans to build a vessel 450m long (1,476ft), 60m beam (196ft), and with a capacity of 22,000 TEUs. If built, this ship would be the largest seagoing vessel in the world.

Figure 27
Maersk Sealand's container ship *Maersk Davao*, photographed in August 2010. With an overall length of 294m (965ft), a beam of 32.2m (105ft) and a draft of 13.5m (44ft), she is a Panamax class vessel with a capacity of 5,100 TEUs.

Containers ships are normally very easy to identify because of their serried ranks of containers. But even unloaded they are usually very recognisable from their large accommodation block towards the stern, topped by the navigation bridge giving a view over the tops of the containers.

Despite the popularity of container ships, the system has some significant disadvantages. Because of the huge range of goods that can be transported by a single vessel, loading and unloading operations have to be planned in great detail to ensure that they are dealt with in the correct order. At the same time, variations in the weights of different containers pose loading problems to ensure that a loaded vessel is not unstable. Limited visibility from a container vessel's bridge can make manoeuvring in confined waters hazardous, while the exposed nature of the containers at sea make them vulnerable to being lost overboard during bad weather. It is estimated that at any given time there are some 5-6 million containers in transit and that more than 10,000 of them are lost at sea each year, resulting in potential navigational hazards and environmental threats[79].

79   See also Q47.

67 What are Pure Car Carriers?

Pure car carriers (PCCs) and their close cousins, Pure Car Truck Carriers (PCTCs), are cargo vessels designed specifically, as their names suggest, to transport wheeled vehicles of various sorts. They are invariably RO/RO vessels – that is, roll-on/roll-off – in which the vehicles drive on and off the vessel under their own power over specially designed ramps.

Modern PCCs and PCTCs are very distinctive, and for most people rather unattractive, vessels with a box-like superstructure running the length and breadth of the hull, typically with both a stern ramp and a side ramp for loading and offloading vehicles. The world's first purpose-built PCC, launched in 1973, could carry 4,200 cars, but more modern vessels can carry 7,000 or more vehicles.

The safety record of PCCs and PCTCs is pretty good, particularly because their box-like construction, without openings in the side, reduces their tendency to ship water in bad weather. However, mishaps to them can be dramatic. In December 2002, the 55,000-ton Wallenius Lines car carrier *Tricolor,* loaded with 3,000 luxury cars including BMWs, Volvos and Saabs, collided with a container

Figure 28
A typical slab-sided Pure Car Carrier, in this case the Panamax Century Highway No 3, entering the Panama Canal in January 2007.

ship and sank some 38km (24 miles) east of Ramsgate, Kent. All 24 crew members survived the incident, but the wreck, in only about 25m (82ft) depth of water, presented a significant navigational hazard in this extremely busy waterway.

68 What are bulk carriers?

Bulk carriers, also called bulk freighters or simply 'bulkers', are vessels specifically designed to transport unpackaged 'bulk' cargo, including both dry ones – such as grains (wheat, maize, rice and so on), coal, metal ores, chemicals such as fertiliser, cement, sand and gravel and so on – and liquid ones, such as petroleum, liquefied gas (see Q69) and liquid edibles like vegetable oils and fruit juices. These cargoes are dropped or poured into the vessel's holds using either the ship's own equipment or dockside facilities.

This general class of vessels represents about 40% of the world's merchant fleets and ranges from small, single-hold vessels with a crew of only three or four, to huge ore ships capable of transporting more than 350,000 metric tonnes and carrying a crew of 30 or more.

The bigger ones are usually readily identifiable at sea because of their shape. Their hulls tend to be long and low, with a large accommodation and bridge block near the stern, rather like container ships. But in front of the accommodation block, instead of piles of containers, bulk carriers generally have a characteristic series of tall pillars and crane gantries between the holds to handle the cargo.

69 What are LNG and LPG ships?

These are specialised container ships for the transport of gas in liquid form, either Liquefied Natural Gas (LNG) or Liquefied Petroleum Gas such as propane or butane (LPG). To liquefy it, the gas has to be cooled to a very low temperature – somewhere around -260°F (-162°C) – when it condenses to the liquid form and occupies only about one six-hundredth of its normal volume as gas. In this form it is stored in huge tanks in the container ships, some of which can carry upwards of 200,000 cubic metres (7,000,000 cubic ft) of gas. There are hundreds of these vessels wandering around the oceans and, with the demand for gas continuing to increase, both their number and size are set to rise.

Some LNG/LPG ships look reasonably conventional, with flattish decks quite similar to bulk carriers. But they also include some of the strangest vessels afloat, characterised by a series of huge domes sticking high above the ship's rails. To make them even more noticeable, they are frequently painted in somewhat garish colours, often orange. And most of them also have LNG or LPG painted in huge letters along the side of the hull so that onlookers can be in no doubt about what they are carrying. This is because liquefied gas is very dangerous stuff and if the structure of the ship's tanks were to be damaged in any way, accidentally or intentionally, the potential for horrific consequences is huge. Consequently, quite a few ports around the world refuse to allow them to dock, particularly because they are considered to be especially vulnerable to terrorist attacks. I would stay well away from them if I were you.

70 What are Suezmax and Panamax ships?

The term 'Suezmax' refers to the largest vessels capable of transiting the Suez Canal fully loaded. 'Panamax', would you believe, is used in much the same way for vessels transiting the Panama Canal, though Suezmax is applied almost exclusively to tankers.

Since the Suez Canal, unlike the Panama Canal, has no locks, the main limiting factor for a transiting vessel is its draft – that is, the depth below the waterline – and its superstructure height, limited to 68m (223ft) by the Suez Canal Bridge.

The current depth of the canal allows for the passage of vessels with a maximum draft of 16m (53ft), though it is currently being deepened and from 2010 the maximum draft is expected to be 22m (72ft). This will allow the passage of fully laden supertankers, which currently have to discharge part of their cargo before transiting the canal.

For vessels wanting to transit the Panama Canal, the controlling factor is the size of the canal's lock chambers, each 320m (1,050ft) long, 33.53m (110ft) wide and 25.9m (85ft) deep. In addition, there is a height restriction imposed by the Bridge of the Americas, which crosses the canal at Bilbao. As a result, the maximum dimensions allowed for a ship transiting the canal are: length 294.1m (965ft); beam 32.3m (106ft), draft 12m (39.5ft); height above the waterline 57.91m (190ft).

These restrictions may be slightly exceeded under very special circumstances, so that the widest ships ever to transit the canal were the American battleships USS *North Carolina* and USS *Washington* with beams of 33.025m (108ft 3.875in), giving a clearance of less than one foot on either side!

Figure 29
Container ship *Hyundai Glory* passing through the Panama Canal in January 2007.
Built in 2004, the vessel is 282m (925ft) long (compared with the Panamax limit of
294.1m/965ft). However, with a beam of 32m (105ft), she is only 10cm (about 4in)
less than the maximum width – as is fairly obvious from this photograph.

Since many vessels afloat, including most supertankers and container ships with
a capacity of more than about 5,000 TEUs, exceed the Panamax dimensions, the
Panama Canal Authority is planning to expand the canal. The expansion will cost
an estimated $5.3 billion and should be completed by 2014. The new set of locks
will be 426.27m (1,400ft) long, 54.86m (180ft) wide and 18.29m (60ft) deep and,
when completed, will be able to deal with vessels up to a capacity of 12,000 TEUs.

VI
Rubbish in the Oceans

It is difficult to sail anywhere in the world ocean without becoming painfully aware that the surface waters, at least, carry an enormous amount of human rubbish. Anything from small bits of plastic, through children's beach balls and fishing floats, to wooden pallets, great balks of timber and complete 12m (40ft) long containers (see Q66) can be – and from time to time are – encountered by cruise ships as they sail the seas. And these are just the bigger things, easily visible from the deck of a moving ship many metres above the water surface. You can bet your bottom dollar that for every visible lump of rubbish there will be dozens of smaller bits and pieces that are too small to be noticed. Even more sinister, you don't have to be an Einstein to realise that at an even more microscopic level the seas contain lots of nasty man-originated chemicals, which from time to time result in horrific scare stories about possible contamination of seafood. Some of this stuff simply falls into the ocean from the land or, like plastic bags, is blown into it. Another lot can originate far from the sea and be carried down by rivers. You only have to sail through the mouth of a relatively small river like the Thames to realise how much man-made rubbish must be carried to the seas each year by the world's really big rivers flowing through densely populated areas. And the oceans generously give much of this land-derived rubbish back to us in the form of shoreline litter that despoils many of our beaches[80]. But a lot of the rubbish in the open ocean was carried there by ships and either fell overboard or was washed over in bad weather or intentionally thrown over the side by the ship's crew.

---

80   A report on *Marine Litter in the North-East Atlantic*, published by OSPAR in 2009, reported levels of beach litter around the North Sea and the Bay of Biscay ranging from 100 to 1,400 items per 100m (330ft) of beach surveyed. They also quote anecdotal evidence from local authorities in France suggesting that an average of about 30 tonnes of marine litter are collected annually from each kilometre of coastline.

Half a century ago, hardly anybody seemed very concerned about this. After all, sailors had always dumped their rubbish over the side, and the general view was that the oceans are so big that they could pretty well take anything that was thrown at or into them without causing much of a problem. And I am ashamed to admit that when I started to go to sea professionally in the early 1970s, my shipmates and I were happy to throw more or less anything over the side without giving it a second thought, despite the fact that we belonged to the Natural Environment Research Council.

Thankfully, things changed dramatically in the next 20 years, and by the 1990s NERC ships were sporting graphic posters in all strategic positions declaring that 'over the side is over', effectively meaning that we threw nothing over the side, but took absolutely all our waste ashore for disposal on land. Without looking into the situation in any great detail, I was reasonably happy with this state of affairs and assumed that the non-dumping practice was more or less universal and was backed up by fairly strict international legislation. Having subsequently been asked lots of questions about what you can and can't throw over the side of a ship, and who decides this, I now know that there is a plethora of national and international organisations with remits to monitor and regulate man's impact on the oceans – and almost as many pressure groups, like Greenpeace and Friends of the Earth, looking over their corporate shoulders. Perhaps not surprisingly in such a complex environment, despite lots of high level discussions and reams of reports and recommendations leading to legislation, it is still not very easy to answer the seemingly simple question, 'What can legally be thrown over the side of a ship at sea?' The next few sections attempt to explain why this should be.

71 What is the International Maritime Organization?[81]

The International Maritime Organization[82] (IMO) is an agency of the United Nations with 169 member states ranging alphabetically from Albania and Algeria to Yemen and Zimbabwe, including such notably maritime nations as Luxembourg and Nepal! It is based in London, housed in a huge brick and glass building at the southern end of Lambeth Bridge, and has an international staff of about 300.

IMO was established in Geneva in 1948 as part of the wide-ranging discussions about the new world order after the Second World War. It met first in 1959 with

---

81   Much of the information in this item is taken from IMO's excellent website: http://www.imo.org
82   The original name was the Inter-Governmental Maritime Consultative Organisation (or IMCO), but the name was changed in 1982.

the general remit of establishing an international regulatory framework for world shipping, particularly all aspects of safety. To do so, it was to produce recommendations and guidance for best practice, as well as regulations to be adhered to by all vessels associated with the signatory nations.

Although safety at sea was, and remains, IMO's primary concern, from its very beginning its remit included the control and prevention of pollution from ships. Throughout the 1960s there was growing concern about the amount of oil being transported by sea and the pollution resulting from tankers cleaning out their tanks. But these concerns paled into insignificance when the supertanker *Torrey Canyon* was wrecked off the coast of Cornwall, England in March 1967 spilling 120,000 tonnes of oil, contaminating almost 300km (185 miles) of the French and British coasts and causing extensive ecological damage.

Over the next few years IMO introduced a series of measures to try to prevent tanker accidents and minimise their consequences, as well as tackling the globally even bigger problem of tank cleaning and the disposal of engine room waste. The most important of these measures was the International Convention for the Prevention of Pollution from Ships, 1973, modified in 1978 to become MARPOL 73/78, the name it is known by today. MARPOL covers not only oil pollution, but also pollution by chemicals, sewage, garbage and packaged goods dumped into the sea, as well as smoke and fumes of all sorts emitted by ships into the air.

Although IMO produces reams of reports and statistics on the basis of which it *adopts* legislation, the organisation has no power or remit to *implement* the rules. Implementation is entirely the responsibility of the member governments and, as IMO's website admits, 'some countries lack the expertise, experience and resources necessary to do this properly'. 'Others,' it says, 'perhaps put enforcement fairly low down on their list of priorities.' Furthermore, the absolute powers of individual governments to implement any legislation is limited under the United Nations Convention on the Law of the Sea (UNCLOS), and in practical terms absolutely no legislation can be implemented on the high seas (that is, beyond the world's Exclusive Economic Zones) other than by military force. Hence the problems there have been with Somali pirates!

72 What is MARPOL?

MARPOL (standing for Marine Pollution) is the main international convention (ie agreement) produced by the International Maritime Organisation (IMO, (see Q71), covering the prevention of pollution of the sea by ships. It is the combination of two separate treaties originally adopted in 1973 and 1978, which have been modified and updated many times since[83]. It currently includes the following six technical annexes, each dealing with a distinct section of the overall problem of pollution by ships at sea.

Annex I   Regulations for the prevention of pollution by oil.
Annex II   Regulations for the control of pollution by noxious liquid substances in bulk.
Annex III   Prevention of pollution by harmful substances carried by sea in packaged form.
Annex IV   Prevention of pollution by sewage from ships.
Annex V   Prevention of pollution by garbage from ships.
Annex VI   Prevention of air pollution from ships.

Interestingly, while all participating states are expected to accept Annexes I and II, acceptance of the other annexes is voluntary!

These annexes are incredibly detailed and tedious to read, but I will try to distil what I think are the most important bits.

Annex I originally came into force in 1983 and its most recent amendment entered into force in 2007. Its most important features are first, that it restricts both the total amount of oil that any vessel may discharge at sea (depending on its size) and limits the rate of such discharge to no more than 30 litres' (6.6 gallons) per nautical mile travelled. Second, it decrees that no discharge of any oil whatsoever must be made from the cargo spaces of a tanker within 80km (50 miles) of the nearest land. The annex also recognises several 'Special Areas' within which the regulations are stricter or discharge of oil wastes is totally disallowed[84].

Annex II identified some 250 substances that, if discharged into the sea, are considered to be potentially harmful either to the marine environment or to humans. These substances must either be discharged into suitable reception facilities or discharged only after having been diluted to below maximum concentrations, depending on the substance. In any case, none of these substances

---

83   This section is based on the latest published version of the regulations *MARPOL Consolidated Edition 2006'*. Its dust cover blurb says that it 'includes the texts of the Convention and its Protocols, Annexes I–VI, Unified Interpretations agreed with the International Association of Classification Societies, and prospective amendments to Annexes I and IV. The text includes all amendments in force as of 22 November 2006 and the revised texts of Annexes I and II (adopted in October 2004), which will enter into force on 1 January 2007'.

84   These special areas are regions 'where for technical reasons in relation to its oceanographical and ecological condition and to the particular character of its traffic, the adoption of special mandatory methods for the prevention of sea pollution is required' (*Marpol, Consolidated Edition 2006*, p47). They include the Mediterranean Sea area, the Baltic Sea area, the Black Sea area, the Red Sea area, the Gulf of Aden area, the Oman Sea area, the North West European Waters and the Antarctic area.

must be discharged within 19.3km (12 miles) of the nearest land and a water depth of not less than 25m (82ft).

Annex III deals mainly with the packaging, labelling and storage of harmful substances during ship transport. It totally prohibits the discharge or jettisoning of these substances 'except where necessary for the purpose of securing the safety of the ship or saving life at sea'.

The current version of Annex IV, the discharge of sewage, originally came into force on 1 August 2005 and applied then to new ships of at least 400 gross tonnage or certified to carry more than 15 persons. But since the annex required existing ships to comply with the regulations within five years of the enforcement date, it applies to all relevant ships from August 2010. It requires all ships to be equipped with either a sewage treatment plant, or a sewage comminuting[85] and disinfecting system, or a sewage holding tank. Where a ship has an approved treatment plant or comminuting and disinfecting system, it may discharge the resulting material as long as it is more than 3nm from the nearest land, while sewage not comminuted and disinfected must not be discharged less than 12nm from the nearest land. However, even then '...sewage that has been stored in holding tanks shall not be discharged instantaneously but at a moderate rate when the ship is en route at not less than 4 knots...' Finally, whatever the circumstances, '...the effluent shall not produce visible floating solids in, nor cause discoloration of, the surrounding water ...' But a final little let-out clause says that the regulations 'shall not apply to ships operating in the waters under the jurisdiction of a State and visiting ships from other States while they are in these waters and are discharging sewage in accordance with less stringent requirements as may be imposed by such State'. In other words, you can do what the devil you like in your own back yard!

Annex V, governing the discharge of garbage, includes all kinds of food, domestic and operational waste, excluding fresh fish, generated during the normal operation of the vessel. The 'fresh fish' bit is presumably there to allow fishermen to throw over the side any of their catches that they don't want to keep, for whatever reason. The annex specifies the distance from land and the manner in which the different types of waste may be disposed of and its regulations apply to all ships. Its most important regulation is the absolute prohibition of the disposal into the sea of all plastics '...including, but not limited to synthetic ropes, synthetic fishing nets and plastic garbage bags ...'. Beyond this, Annex V insists that all discharge of garbage into the sea should take place as far as practicable from the nearest land but then goes on to establish several more specific requirements. Thus, 'dunnage[86]', lining and packing materials

---

85   That is, pulverising into tiny pieces.
86   'Dunnage' refers to pieces of timber traditionally used to secure cargo or items of deck equipment to prevent it moving in rough weather.

which will float' should not be discharged less than 25nm from the nearest land. On the other hand 'food wastes and all other garbage including paper products, rags, glass, metal, bottles, crockery and similar refuse' should not be discharged less than 12nm from the nearest land - except that, if it has been ground up into pieces no bigger than 25mm (that is about an inch) across, they can be discharged as long as the vessel is more than 3 miles from the nearest land.

Like Annex I, Annex V also recognises special areas where the regulations are more stringent. In these areas, basically the same ones identified in footnote 84 but also includes the 'Wider Caribbean Region', not only is the discharge of all plastics prohibited, but so is that of 'paper products, rags, glass, metal, bottles, crockery, dunnage, lining and packing materials'. For some strange reason, whereas ground up food waste can be discharged in the Wider Caribbean Region no closer than 3nm from the nearest land, just like in 'non special' areas, in the rest of these precious bits such discharge must be at least 12m from the nearest land.

Annex VI, concerned with air pollution from ships, is the most detailed of all, dealing with the certification of vessels in order to testify to the acceptability, from a polluting point of view, of their engines and other potentially emitting machinery. It makes a particular fuss about 'ozone depleting substances', totally prohibiting their emission and even banning the use of installations containing these substances, 'except that new installations containing hydro-chlorofluorocarbons (HCFCs) shall be permitted until 1 January 2020'. Annex VI also specifies the minimum requirements of the fuels to be used for various purposes, particularly the sulphur content. Finally, it includes a large section governing incineration at sea, specifying the minimum temperatures for such incineration and banning the incineration of any materials containing polychlorinated biphenols (PCBs) or significant quantities of heavy metals or halogen compounds. The incineration of polyvinyl chlorides (PVCs) is also prohibited, unless the vessel is provided with an IMO approved incinerator.

Interestingly, ships are allowed to burn their own sewage sludge or engine-generated sludge oil in their power plants or boilers except while the vessel is inside a port, harbour or estuary.

73   What is echo-sounding?

Echo-sounding is a technique used to determine the depth of the sea based on the fact that sound travels much more efficiently, and quickly, through water than it does through air. By sending a narrow beam of sound towards the seafloor from a floating vessel, and measuring very accurately the time interval between the propagation of the sound signal and the return of its echo bounced back from the seabed, it is possible to calculate the depth.

The 'sounding' part of the term doesn't, as you might expect, refer to the noise or sound used in the process. Instead, it comes from an old anglo-saxon word *sond* meaning something like messenger, from which we get the modern expression 'to sound someone or something out', possibly by sending a messenger to assess the situation for us. The same root gave the verb 'to sound' meaning to determine the depth or, applied to whales, to dive into the depths.

From the very earliest days of navigation the depth of water beneath a ship's keel was measured simply by lowering a weighted rope over the vessel's side. The depth was then determined by noting which of a series of marks along the rope's length was nearest to the surface when the weight was on the bottom and the rope was vertical. The weight on the end of a sounding line would originally have been any handy stone or lump of iron, but eventually it metamorphosed into a regularly shaped piece of lead, and the line became known as a leadline. When ships were navigating in waters where the depth was uncertain it was normal for a 'leadsman' to stand on a small platform near the front of the ship and take regular soundings with a leadline, shouting the results to the officer of the watch[87]. And because this job was considered by the other sailors, rather unjustifiably, to be a fairly easy one it gave rise to the expression 'swinging the lead' as a euphemism for avoiding hard work.

The standard leadline used on most vessels would be no more than 100 fathoms, that is 600ft or rather less than 200m long, with a standard system of marks along its length. If a line of this length didn't reach to the seabed, there was little likelihood of dangerously shallow water in the vicinity and most ship's masters had no further interest in determining the depth. But during the nineteenth century interest in measuring the depth of the deep ocean grew rapidly, particularly with the development of submarine telegraphy for which knowledge of the shape and nature of the seafloor was crucial. The old leadline technique went through a whole series of developments to adapt it for use in deep water, including using thinner and thinner lines and eventually wire to reduce its resistance in the water. At the same time, increasingly ingenious mechanical techniques were also developed to release the heavy weights once they had reached the seabed and enable the light line to retrieve a sample of the bottom sediment. But despite all this ingenuity the weighted

---

87 This sounding technique was not, of course, restricted to seagoing vessels, but was equally important for ships navigating rivers and lakes. The famous American author, Mark Twain, whose real name was Samuel Langhorn Clemens, took his pen name from the call of leadsmen on Mississippi river boats in which the expression 'By the Mark Twain' meant that there was at least two fathoms or six feet of water beneath the vessel and it was therefore safe to proceed.

line technique had a number of serious drawbacks. First, it was extremely labour intensive, especially before steam winches became widely available and the line had to be wound in by manpower alone. Second, even under the best conditions this was a very time-consuming process, a single deep sounding often taking five or six hours to complete. Finally, the results were frequently unreliable, with rough weather and strong currents often making it impossible to determine when the weight reached the bottom. As a result, lots of extremely dodgy depth measurements were reported and reliable knowledge of the shape of the ocean basins accumulated very slowly indeed. Echo-sounding eventually came to the rescue, but it took a long time.

There were a number of unsuccessful attempts to use sound for depth determination during the 19th century, but the development of modern echo-sounding was spurred on by the loss of the *Titanic* in 1912 when a number of independent workers tried to develop sonic methods of detecting icebergs and determining how far away they were. The technique proved to be fairly useless for detecting icebergs, but very effective in determining the water depth.

Early echo-sounding depended on single sharp sounds being produced, often by simply banging one piece of metal against another, and an operator wearing earphones connected to a hydrophone on the ship's hull listening for the return of the echo. Although this meant that a single deep sounding might take several seconds, the improvement over the old sounding line technique which could take hours was huge and well worth pursuing. Consequently, the technology was refined over the next few decades and particularly during and after the Second World War. As a result, a huge range of sophisticated instruments is now available ranging from small, battery-powered short-range sounders for yachts and similar small vessels, to extremely accurate echo-sounders with full ocean depth capability used by research vessels. In fact, most cruise ships are now fitted with powerful echo-sounders so that the captain's daily report almost invariably includes a seemingly precise statement of the depth under the vessel's keel.

Actually, the captain's statement is probably not quite as accurate as it sounds. His echo-sounder reading will almost certainly be based on an assumed speed of sound through seawater close to 1,500 metres per second. For all practical purposes this is fine, and for shallow water soundings it will provide a pretty accurate result. But the speed of sound through water is dependent upon its density, the higher the density the higher the speed. And seawater density depends upon its temperature and salinity. So to produce a really accurate depth of water from an echo-sounder record you need to know the density structure of the water column and apply an appropriate correction. Oceanographers have these corrections available in a series of tables that can make a difference of 20 or 30m in depths of 5,000m or so. Such an 'error' is of no significance to a cruise ship captain, but might be quite crucial for the calculations of a marine physicist.

So far we have dealt only with systems that measure the depth directly beneath the ship's keel, that is providing a line of depths under the ship's track but giving no indication of how the depth might vary on either side of this narrow line. However, the last 40 years or so has seen major advances in echo-sounding technology, particularly in the use of narrow 'sheets' of sound that can be transmitted to either side of the ship's track so that the return echo provides a picture of a whole swathe of the sea bed instead of simply a single line. In fact, the most advanced systems on research vessels can project their sound beams not only to the side but also ahead of the vessel, so that the ship can be forewarned of changes in the shape of the seabed even before they have reached it!

74 What is the Great Pacific Garbage Patch?

The Great Pacific Garbage Patch is a huge area of the North Pacific Ocean containing exceptionally high concentrations of man-made rubbish, particularly bits of plastic.

Although the garbage patch has been known about for more than 20 years, I am ashamed to say that I had never heard of it until a passenger on the *Marco Polo* brought it to my attention as we sailed across the North Atlantic in January 2010. When I got access to the internet, I found that there is an enormous amount written about the patch, some good and some not so good. This item is a distillate of some of this stuff, with some additional bits and pieces that seem relevant.

Apparently, the first clues about the patch's existence came in the late 1980s when Alaska-based marine scientists found high concentrations of plastic rubbish floating at, or close to, the surface in various parts of the North Pacific. They suggested that they were caused by the particular pattern of surface currents, specifically the system known as the North Pacific Gyre. Then, in 1997, ocean sailing boat captain Charles J Moore, returning from Hawaii to California, came across a vast patch of floating rubbish in the gyre and alerted the American oceanographic community and the public. Mr Moore continues to be actively involved in raising the public's awareness of the garbage patch and of marine pollution in general. So why should all this rubbish accumulate in the gyre, and where on earth does it all come from? Let's see if we can unravel it a bit.

The ocean's surface currents, including those of the North Pacific Gyre, were dealt with in some detail in *Do Whales...?*, but here's a brief resumé relevant to the garbage patch story. The combination of the earth's pattern of winds, together with the effects of the rotation of the planet and the distribution of the main land masses, causes a complex circulatory system made up of dozens of currents in the surface waters of the seas; some of these are very strong and more or less permanent, some weak and intermittent – and there is every variation in between. But the basic pattern consists of a series of five huge circular current systems called gyres[88], two in the Atlantic, two in the Pacific and one in the Indian Ocean. These gyres flow in a clockwise direction in the northern hemisphere and anti-clockwise in the southern hemisphere and each consists of several separately named currents, though the boundaries between them are rather blurred.

The most familiar of these gyres, at least to European and North American readers, is that in the North Atlantic, with its western and northern sections being formed by the most famous surface current of them all, the Gulf Stream. It is well known that this huge current, flowing as it does from the warm waters of the tropical western Atlantic, past the eastern seaboard of the United States, to bathe the shores of north-western Europe, transfers huge quantities of heat and ensures that the climate of western Europe is much less extreme than the regions of eastern North America at similar latitudes. After it leaves the North American coast, roughly in the vicinity of Newfoundland, the Gulf Stream splits into two, a southerly branch, flowing towards the east or south-east as the Azores Current and a more northerly one, called the North Atlantic Current or North Atlantic Drift. It is the waters of this northerly branch that warm the coasts of western Ireland and Scotland. But by no means all of the North Atlantic Current flows so far north. Instead, like the Gulf Stream before it, to the west of Ireland the North Atlantic Current splits into a northern and southern branch. The southern branch, called the Canary Current, turns right (that is, towards the south), flows past the coasts of France and the Iberian Peninsula and is joined by the eastward-flowing Azores Current as it flows past the Canary Islands from which it gets its name. Finally, at about 25°N, the current turns to the right yet again, now to flow towards the west as the North Equatorial Current, eventually turning north to the north-west of the Caribbean to form the Gulf Stream and thus complete the loop.

The huge area of ocean enclosed within this circular current system was familiar to the old sailing ship navigators as typified by long periods of calm weather without winds or currents. Since it is also characterised by large floating patches of ship-stopping sargassum weed, more or less trapped like floating rubbish in the middle of a whirlpool, the area became known as the Sargasso Sea (see Q40) and acquired a fearful reputation for being difficult to sail through. All the other ocean gyres have the same wind and current-less characteristics, but because they do not seem to accumulate the same levels of weed, and possibly also because they were not so frequently traversed by sailing vessels,

---

88   The word 'gyre' simply means a turning around or revolution. It is derived from a Latin word, *gyrus*, meaning ring or circle, which, along with gyre, gives us words like gyrate and gyration, as well as all those compound words beginning with *gyro-* like gyrocompass and gyroscope.

they do not seem to have attained quite the same degree of notoriety. Nevertheless, just like the Sargasso Sea, the central regions of all of them would tend to accumulate and trap floating material such as plant matter fallen or blown into the ocean from land areas and, of course, stuff washed or thrown overboard from ships. And the Pacific Garbage Patch seems to be a dramatic and extreme version of the same phenomenon.

The Pacific Ocean covers an area of about 166 million km^2 (64 million square miles), almost twice that of the Atlantic, and the North Pacific Gyre, with the Hawaiian archipelago at its centre, is correspondingly much bigger than its Atlantic counterpart (some 34 million km^2/13 million square miles compared with only about 3 million km^2/1.15 million square miles). However, just like the Sargasso Sea, the North Pacific Gyre is surrounded by a clockwise-flowing series of currents: the north-east flowing Kuroshio Current in the west, the North Pacific Current in the north, the California Current flowing southwards off the western seaboard of North America and finally the westward-flowing Pacific North Equatorial Current, forming the southern boundary and completing the loop. And just as the currents in the North Atlantic are responsible for trapping the sargassum weed, it seems that the equivalent currents in the North Pacific are the culprits trapping the rubbish in the garbage patch.

Just how big the garbage patch is, and how much rubbish it contains, is still very uncertain. Estimates range from about 1 million to 15 million km^2 (386,000–5.8 million square miles), with a load of up to 100 million tons of debris. But much of the evidence on which these estimates are based is anecdotal – that is, derived from fairly unsystematic, albeit careful, observations by non-specialists such as recreational navigators as they traverse the patch, much as Charles Moore did in 1997. Furthermore, although the patch contains a distressing amount of large and easily visible rubbish like plastic bags and bottles, netting and so on, much of it seems to be in the form of tiny particles of plastic no more than a few millimetres across and difficult to see and collect without specialist equipment.

Fortunately, our knowledge of the patch is likely to improve rapidly in the next few years with the establishment of a collaborative research programme by scientists from Japan and the USA to study the patch. Named Project Kaisei (Japanese for 'ocean planet'), the first scientific cruise devoted to the study of the patch took place in August 2009 when specialists from the Scripps Institution of Oceanography in San Diego, California, took many samples from the surface waters over a 2,200km (1,367 mile) tack through the gyre[89]. The detailed results will take

---

89   The cruise was called SEAPLEX, standing for Scripps Environmental Accumulation of Plastic Expedition. If you look this up on the web you will find lots of fascinating stuff about the programme and the results.

many months to appear, but the expedition confirmed the serious nature of the problem and some of the characteristics of the rubbish.

The bulk of the material is in the form of tiny confetti-like bits of plastic, frequently referred to as 'nurdles' (see Q75), floating in the upper 10m (33ft) or so. It is estimated that some 80% of it comes from land sources, mainly from the west coast of North America and the east coast of Asia, and the remainder from ships.

The effect of the garbage patch on the marine ecosystem is still largely unknown, though it has been the subject of some very alarmist claims. There are certainly serious consequences resulting from marine creatures being caught up in plastic netting and lines of various sorts, and of others, particularly turtles and seabirds, ingesting plastic bags and sheeting. There may well be other, less obvious, impacts by the small plastic particles and the chemicals derived from their breakdown. But much more research is required before the magnitude of these effects, including the potential effects on humans, can be assessed.

Whatever the results of these studies, it is very unlikely that the Pacific Garbage Patch will turn out to be unique. Instead, it is almost certain that similar, albeit possibly less dramatic, patches of man-made rubbish will be found in at least some of the ocean's other major gyres[90].

75 What are nurdles?

Nurdles, or possibly somewhat more properly 'pre-production plastic pellets', are tiny pieces of plastic, or polyethylene, typically less than about 5mm (¼in) in diameter, which make up the raw material from which all manner of plastic articles, ranging from bottles and food containers to plastic bags and even clothes, are eventually manufactured.

Nurdles are a by-product of the petroleum industry and are considered a convenient form in which to transport polyethylene from the source to the plastic goods manufacturing plants, because they can be packed easily into any convenient container and readily moved using vacuum hoses and hoppers. As a result, about 100 million tonnes of nurdles are shipped around the world each year, mostly in huge rail and sea containers. Individually, nurdles are very light, with about 50–60,000 in a kilogram (25,000 in a pound). Not surprisingly, lots of nurdles

---

90 And just after I had written this, in April 2010, reports began to appear that masses of small particles of plastic, similar to those found in the Pacific Garbage Patch, had been collected by two groups of American scientists in the North Atlantic.

escape during transport, just like those irritating bits of polystyrene packing do whenever you open a box containing something the manufacturer thought was particularly precious. Some of these escapes occur on or close to the sea, for example in harbours. But even those that are lost far from the ocean are mostly transported eventually to the sea by a combination of wind and water. As a result, they are estimated to make up about 10% of all the litter washed up on beaches around the world in recent years, and presumably also of the plastic rubbish in the central parts of the oceans, such as the Pacific Garbage Patch (see Q74).

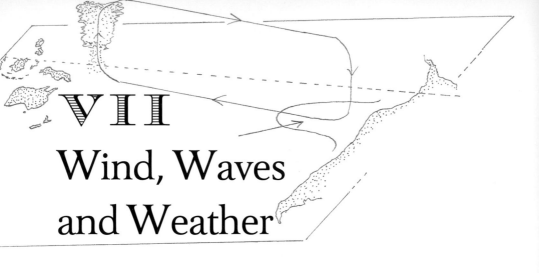

VII
Wind, Waves and Weather

76 What causes all those strange marks on the surface of the ocean?

When the sea is calm, the surface is usually anything but monotonously uniform. Instead, it is often covered in strange patches and streaks, sometimes apparently totally irregular, sometimes in more or less straight lines. So what on earth causes them?

Well, there are lots of possible reasons, some extremely simple, some more complex. Here are a few of them.

The simplest explanation for dark patches on the ocean surface are, would you believe, the shadows of clouds. How basic is that? But it is not always quite as obvious as you might think, and cloud shadows have certainly misled me a few times.

Two or three decades ago it was quite common to see oil slicks on the ocean surface where passing vessels had accidentally or, all too frequently, intentionally released oil into the sea. This is less common these days, since attitudes to dumping things in the ocean have hardened (see Q72). Nevertheless, oil slicks can still be seen from time to time though, thankfully, rarely in the huge quantities released following the tragic explosion in April 2010 on BP's Deepwater Horizon offshore drilling platform in the Gulf of Mexico.

Other patches of ocean that appear to be different from the rest in colour or 'texture' usually represent different water masses with different characteristics, albeit sometimes very slight. This is because seawaters with different temperatures or saltiness (salinity) don't mix at all easily. Perhaps the most obvious examples of this phenomenon are seen where major rivers enter the sea. The river water is often carrying a load of suspended mud or sand, which give it a very distinctive appearance. Patches of such water can often be seen far out to sea, sometimes hundreds of miles in the case of very big rivers like the Amazon[91].

On a much smaller scale, currents, including tidal currents, can cause differences in the appearance of the water by bringing together waters of different characteristics. On a large scale, the waters of major currents like the Gulf Steam can be very distinct from the waters on either side, producing clear boundaries between them. In shallow water, currents can also produce strange 'whirlpool' effects, usually caused by water being forced upwards by an underwater feature such as a submerged hill.

But among the more intriguing surface marks are the more or less straight lines that sometimes go on for miles. When these are single lines of light or dark water several metres wide across an otherwise fairly featureless sea, they often turn out to be the maritime equivalent of vapour trails. As any powered vessel moves through the water, it leaves a wake behind it, caused partly by the disturbance produced by the ship's hull but also by the churning effect of the propeller or propellers. Much of the distinct appearance of the wake immediately behind the vessel is caused by tiny bubbles of air suspended in the churned-up water. Most of these bubbles rise to the surface and burst fairly quickly, so that by the time the wake is a few tens of metres behind the ship a good deal of the whiteness will have disappeared. Nevertheless, the wake will still be quite distinct well into the distance – so why is this? It is simply because the water brought to the surface by the propellers will be subtly different from the surface water itself, and depending on the conditions these differences may persist for minutes or even hours after the ship has passed. Big ships can bring water to the surface from depths of more than 10m (33ft), along with their populations of plankton and other small creatures. This is why sea surface feeding seabirds, particularly terns, follow ships and actively feed on the resulting bonanza. But long after the birds have flown off, either because they have eaten all the stirred-up food morsels or because the morsels have gone back down well below the surface, the stirred-up water is likely to stay visible for a long time, hence the trail.

Finally, we come to windrows. These are streaks in the water up to a metre or so wide but extending hundreds of metres across the ocean as lines marked by foam, floating seaweed (see Fig 30) or all sorts of other bits of debris like plastic bottles and the like. They occur in groups of up to a hundred or more parallel lines, usually between 40 and 50m (130–165ft) apart and lined up with the wind (see Fig 31).

91   Amazon visitors will be well aware that a similar phenomenon of distinct waters not mixing quickly can be seen within the river system itself. Three distinct types of river are recognisable within the Amazonian basin, depending mainly on the underlying geology in their headwaters. Because of their resulting appearance they are called black, white or clear water rivers. Where they come together in the main river, the waters of different origins flowing alongside one another can remain distinct for many miles.

Figure 30
A typical windrow, in this case made up of bits of sargassum weed in the North
Atlantic in January 2010.

They are caused by a phenomenon called Langmuir circulation, after an American Nobel prize-winning physicist, Irving Langmuir, who proposed it in the 1930s as an explanation for windrows of sargassum weed that he had seen in the Sargasso Sea (see Q40). It seems that as the wind blows across the surface of the sea, it sets up helical or spiral movements in the upper layers down to depths of 5–10m (16–33ft) and 20–25m (65–82ft) wide. Adjacent spirals flow in opposite directions so that every 40–50m (130–165ft) or so there will be a strip of ocean where the water in two adjacent spirals is flowing upwards and then diverging at the surface. About halfway between these *divergent* regions the opposite situation will occur, with water from adjacent spirals *converging* and then sinking to form the deeper parts of the spirals. Anything floating at the surface will naturally be carried to the converging strips, where they will accumulate to form the familiar windrows. A very similar process occurs in the lower atmosphere, but on a much bigger scale, producing the so-called cloud streets[92] in which clouds are lined up in long parallel lines.

92   For more good stuff on Irving Langmuir and on all aspects of clouds, see Gavin Pretor-Pinney's excellent *The Cloudspotter's Guide*, Hodder and Stoughton, 2006.

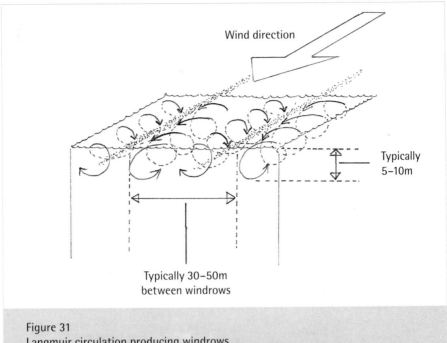

Wind direction

Typically
5–10m

Typically 30–50m
between windrows

Figure 31
Langmuir circulation producing windrows.

77 What is El Niño?

El Niño, or more properly the El Niño Southern Oscillation (ENSO), is a climatic
phenomenon linking the surface waters of the Pacific Ocean and the overlying
atmosphere. It results in an alternation between two contrasting climatic situations,
with one of these, the El Niño proper, occurring every two to ten years. Although
its most dramatic effects are restricted to the tropical Pacific, it can have much
more widespread consequences. For example, as far as the oceans are concerned,
it can cause an increase of global surface water temperatures of a few tenths of
a degree Celsius over a timescale of a year or so, comparable to the change
attributed to the huge increase in atmospheric carbon dioxide over the last century.

The name El Niño (meaning the Christ child) comes from the fact that one of
the key features indicating the onset of the phenomenon is a sudden warming of
the surface waters off the north-western coast of South America; in the late 19th
century the local fishermen noticed that this occurred usually around Christmas
time – hence the name. An El Niño event can last just a few weeks and have
relatively minor consequences, or it can last for a year or more with much more
significant and widespread results.

To understand exactly what happens in an El Niño event we need first to look, very briefly, at the earth's climate more generally. In *Do Whales...?* (Q98), I gave a greatly simplified overview of the earth's climate, pointing out that it is dominated by a series of alternately high and low pressure zones circling the earth parallel to the equator. In this system the equatorial zone and the sub-polar zones at roughly 60° north and south are characterised by low pressure, while the subtropical regions at about 30° north and south are usually characterised by high pressure. This system, together with the effect of the earth's rotation, produces a series of atmospheric 'cells' in which winds blow at low altitudes from the high pressure to the low pressure areas and then return in the opposite direction at high altitudes.

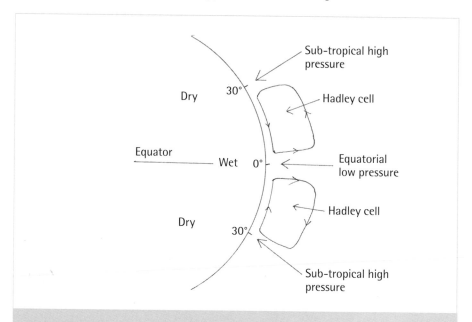

Figure 32
Section through the earth showing the two Hadley cells on either side of the equator, named for the 18th-century British meteorologist who first predicted their existence. In this simplified diagram the cells appear to be oriented north–south. In fact, because of the rotation of the earth the cells are skewed to the right (that is, to the south-west) in the northern hemisphere and to the left (the north-west) in the southern hemisphere (see Fig 33).

Fig 32 illustrates two of these cells, the Hadley cells on either side of the equator, that are mainly responsible for the typical pattern of north-easterly and south-easterly 'trade' winds respectively to the north and south of the equator in both the Atlantic and Pacific oceans. They are also the reason that the tropics are generally very wet, while the earth's deserts are concentrated around 30–40° north and south of the equator. This is because the warm moist air brought towards the equator by the trade winds rises in the tropics and cools down. As it does so it typically produces impressive cumulonimbus clouds (Fig 33), towering tens of thousands of feet above the surface and dumping their load of water in huge downpours. Having lost its water, the high altitude air now moves in the opposite direction to the low altitude trade winds, eventually to sink once more as cool, very dry air at around 30°N and 30°S and thus complete the Hadley cell.

Figure 33
Cumulonimbus cloud in the process of dumping its water, photographed in the Atlantic close to the equator in March 2008. For much more information on cumulonimbus clouds and all the others, see Gavin Pretor-Pinney's *The Cloudspotter's Guide.*

In the 'normal' or 'non-El Niño' atmospheric situation in the region (see Fig 34), there is a high-pressure area over the eastern subtropical Pacific and a low-pressure area over northern Australia and Indonesia. South-east trade winds blow between the two areas, picking up heat and moisture from the sea surface as they do so. By the time they reach the western Pacific these winds are warm and wet, and because the air is so warm it rises and cools, dropping its moisture as rain. The cooler, drier air now moves back towards the south-east at high altitude as part of a Hadley cell (see *Do Whales...?* Q114) and completes the circulation by sinking off the west coast of South America to reinforce the high-pressure area again.

Apart from determining the distribution of rainfall in the area, the trade winds also have a dramatic effect on the sea by causing a westward-flowing surface current more or less along the equator. The water flowing in this current away from the north-western coasts of South America is replaced by cold, nutrient-rich water upwelling from depths of several hundreds of metres. In turn, the upwelling nutrients stimulate the growth of phytoplankton, zooplankton and all the higher levels in the food chain including fish, mammals and birds.

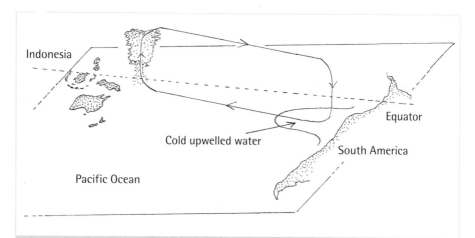

Figure 34
Diagram showing the 'normal' (that is, the non-El Niño) situation, in the tropical southern Pacific. The Hadley cell causes south-easterly trade winds to blow across the Pacific from the north-western coasts of South America towards Australasia and Indonesia. This results in rain in Indonesia and upwelling of cold, nutrient-rich water off the coasts of Ecuador and Peru.

For reasons still not fully understood, this 'normal' situation periodically breaks down and the high- and low-pressure areas essentially reverse their positions. As a result, both the south-east trade winds and the westward-flowing surface current weaken, slowing or stopping the upwelling of cold water. Consequently, the temperature of the surface waters in the eastern central Pacific increases by as much as 5°C (9°F) as warmer equatorial waters move in. An important positive consequence is that the normally very dry eastern Pacific receives much needed rainfall during these El Niño episodes, while northern Australasia and Indonesia experience unusually dry weather. However, a much more serious consequence is that the loss of nutrient-rich upwelling water results in a major decrease in the growth of phytoplankton which, in turn, has a huge impact on fish and seabird populations.

The non-El Niño situation, now increasingly referred to as La Niña, is the reason for the huge productivity of this east Pacific region, including the enormous populations of seabirds that, over many generations, produced vast deposits of guano – that is, phosphate- and nitrate-rich deposits of bird faeces exploited from the mid-19th century to the late 20th century for use as agricultural fertiliser. The birds feed on the normally abundant populations of marine invertebrates and fish, including the Peruvian anchovy, which became the target of a major fishery from the late 1950s onwards. It grew very rapidly, reaching an annual harvest of around 10 million tonnes per year after about 15 years. But at that time relatively little was known about the effects of an El Niño, nor how to forecast one, so the anchovy fishery collapsed in the early 1970s, mainly because of two serious El Niño years in quick succession. It took more than 20 years for the fishery to recover to a comparable level to that before the collapse. In the meantime, much more research has been conducted into the causes and broader geographical consequences of El Niño events, particularly their influence on the weather in Africa, where they are associated with increased rainfall, and in Eurasia and North America, where they seem to be linked to extremely cold winters.

In part as a response to a series of strong El Niño events and the realisation of the importance of being able to forecast them, there has been a major international programme since the early 1990s to study the ocean-atmosphere interaction in the tropical Pacific. This programme, called the Tropical Atmosphere Ocean (TAO) project, is funded jointly by the USA, Japan and France, who all have major interests in the region. An important feature of the project is an array of about 70 deep ocean moorings scattered across the equatorial Pacific and carrying instruments that gather oceanographic data, including water temperature and current profiles, and send them back to shore-based observing stations via satellites. The hope is that this array will not only provide ocean scientists with early warnings of the onset of significant El Niño events, but also help in an understanding of how the oceans and atmosphere interact in this and other geographical regions of the earth.

78 What causes marine mirages?

All mirages, over land or sea, are caused by light rays from distant objects being bent, or refracted, as they pass through layers of air of different densities, usually because of temperature variations. The result is that when the rays reach an observer's eyes they make the object seem to be displaced and either much closer, or further away, than they really are.

Under so-called 'normal' atmospheric conditions the air above the land or the sea gets gradually cooler with increasing altitude, the temperature falling fairly gently at a rate of about 1°C for every 100 metres or so of height. Under these conditions light rays travel in rather straight lines and we see things more or less as they really are. But these normal conditions can be disturbed by the local conditions producing one or other of two quite distinct temperature distributions, each resulting in specific types of mirage.

The classic movie mirage in which travellers across the desert see what looks like water some distance ahead of them, but can never reach it, is caused by the hot sand heating up the thin layer adjacent to it. If the top of this very warm layer is below the observer's eye line it can bend light rays coming from the sky so that they appear to be coming from the sand itself and fooling the thirsty traveller's mind into thinking that he is seeing water (see Fig 35a).

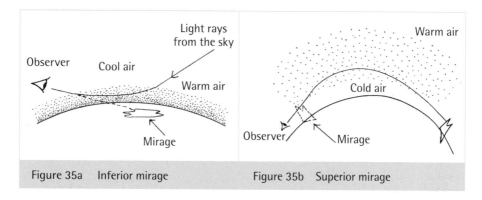

Figure 35a   Inferior mirage   Figure 35b   Superior mirage

The same phenomenon can be seen in any very sunny situation where the air is over an expanse of hot surface such as a long straightish road. The dark road surface will absorb the sun's heat and radiate it back to the thin layer of air immediately above its surface, just like the desert sand. And in exactly the same way, a traveller coming along the road will commonly see what appears to be shimmering pools of water covering the road in the distance but is actually a bit of the sky from above the horizon. The images produced by this type of mirage are called *inferior* ones, not referring to their quality, but simply indicating that the appearance of the displaced object, the sky in the above examples, is below its true position. This type of mirage at sea can make a section of sky appear beneath the horizon producing a very peculiar effect (see Fig 36).

In contrast, the second non-normal temperature distribution, with relatively warm air overlying a thin layer of much colder air on the surface, produces so-called *superior* images because they are physically above the object's true position. This type of mirage is probably most commonly seen at sea and can make ships or pieces of land visible even though they are technically out of the direct line of sight beneath the horizon. This is because the light rays are bent or refracted downwards rather than upwards as inferior mirages (see Fig 35b) and can often produce inverted images. They can be seen in many parts of the world, but are most common in polar regions. One particularly complex sub-set, known as Fata Morgana, named after Morgan le Fay, the fairy half-sister of King Arthur, can change rapidly including from inverted to erect images in a matter of seconds. The following two pictures are from a series taken near Narsarsuaq, Greenland, in July 2007 in which the passengers on Fred Olsen's *Boudicca* were treated to an incredible display ranging from double images of mountains balancing on their summits, to what appeared to be huge flats across the horizon breaking up and reforming within seconds and, as in Fig 38, just as rapidly turning into lighthouses!

Figure 36
This photo was taken in the English Channel in January 2010 when the sea was considerably warmer than the air. It seems that the light strip beneath the distant ship is actually a piece of sky 'mis-placed' by refraction of the light rays by the thin layer of relatively warm air, just like a desert mirage.

Figure 37   Figure 38

Figure 37
Photo taken over an ice field leaving Narsarsuaq in southwestern Greenland in July 2007. The true horizon is the pale line across the middle of the picture. The line of white cliffs' above the horizon are an inverted image of an icy shoreline over the horizon.

Figure 38
A telephoto view of part of the 'cliffs' in Figure 37, taken about ten minutes later. By this time most of the cliffs' had disappeared, but with part of them replaced by this obvious, but fake, lighthouse. Goodness knows what it actually is, because no structure remotely like this is known in the area.

79 Do volcanoes contribute to global warming?

This is not, strictly speaking, an oceanographic question, though most volcanoes actually erupt under the seas. But it was prompted particularly by the eruption of Iceland's unpronounceable volcano Eyjafjallajökull in March–April 2010, causing a major disruption to commercial air traffic and prompting a rethink of the rules governing flight restrictions imposed by the civil aviation authorities.

In the past I have been asked the question several times, particularly by global-warming cynics. Without really knowing the answer, I said that while I realised that the CO_2 emitted from volcanoes must surely contribute to the total amount of this greenhouse gas in the atmosphere, I thought that they were relatively insignificant compared with some of man's CO_2-generating activities. However, the eruption of Eyjafjallajökull has replaced my ignorance with a modicum of hard evidence, which I will share with you[96].

Apparently, all those cancelled flights represented a decrease in airplane emissions of CO_2 of something like 2 million tonnes, against which the emission of the volcano must be set. The latest figures I have for this is up to June 2010, by which time the total mass of material thrown into the atmosphere was estimated at about one tenth of a cubic kilometre, thought to weigh about 250 million tonnes. Wow, it doesn't look good so far. However, magmas like the one in Iceland can only carry up to about 0.5% of its weight as carbon dioxide. So Eyjafjallajökull seems to have chucked out about 1.25 million tonnes compared with the 2 million 'saved' by reducing the air traffic; a modest 'win' for the volcano, at least up to June.

But this is not the whole story. It is well known that the bulk of the ash thrown out by volcanoes is in the form of very fine particles less than 50 microns (that is 1/20th of a millimetre) across. These particles apparently weather – that is, are broken down and incorporated into soils of various sorts – very rapidly. In the process they lock up, or sequester, a lot of carbon and oxygen as the magnesium and calcium oxides in the ash are weathered to carbonates. Up to June 2010 the best estimate was that the emissions from Eyjafjallajökull would, within a few months, sequester a staggering 19 million tonnes of CO_2, knocking the other figures pretty well into a cocked hat!

---

96   Most of this answer is taken from the June 2010 edition of *Greenhouse Issues,* the house journal of the IEAGHG, an international collaborative programme established in 1991 by the International Energy Agency to investigate technologies to reduce greenhouse gas emissions from the use of fossil fuels.

FURTHER READING

The literature on the world's oceans is vast, with most of it being far too specialised for most of us to be able to read it with anything approaching total
comprehension, let alone pleasure. Here I list only a small number of relatively
recently published books that I believe are both well-written and trustworthy.

Clover, Charles (2005) *The End of the Line, How Fishing is Changing the World
and What We Eat*, Ebury Press, London. An excellent, but very disturbing, read
about the parlous state of world fisheries by the *Daily Telegraph's* environment
correspondent. Includes a useful guide to the fish species that the environmentally
conscientious among us should, and should not, eat.

Dear, ICB and Kemp, Peter [Eds] (2005) *The Oxford Companion to Ships and the
Sea*, Oxford University Press, Oxford. A new and greatly revised edition of an old
and respected reference work on all things maritime.

Fearnley-Whittingstall, Hugh and Fisher, Nick (2007) *The River Cottage Fish Book*,
Bloomsbury Publishing, London. Six hundred pages of extremely lavishly illustrated
salt and freshwater fish stuff. As you might expect from the River Cottage man,
lots of it is devoted to recipes for meals that look unbelievably yummy in the
photos. But it also has a huge amount of good solid information about the biology
of the beasts involved, how they are harvested and how to deal with them if you
get them *au naturel,* so to speak. Finally, like Charles Clover's *The End of the Line,*
F-W and Fisher provide good guidance on what you can eat with a clear conscience.
Good value at the full published price of £30, but I got mine remaindered at a
fraction of that price so I expect there are plenty about.

Hoare, Philip (2009) *Leviathan or, the Whale*, Fourth Estate, London. Lots of good
stuff about whales and whaling – and a very good read. Unfortunately, the repro-
duction of the photos in the paperback edition is truly appalling.

Pretor-Pinney, Gavin (2007) *The Cloudspotter's Guide*, Sceptre, London. All you
ever wanted to know about clouds and the processes producing them, lots of it
relevant to the ocean.

Roberts, Callum (2007) *The Unnatural History of the Sea. The past and future of humanity and fishing*, Gaia, London. A learned, but readable and entertaining account of man's past and present fishing activities. Like Charles Clover's *The End of the Line*, it makes pretty depressing reading, but at least has a touch of optimism at the end.

Summerhayes, CP and Thorpe, SA [Eds] (1996) *Oceanography: An Illustrated Guide*, Manson Publishing, London. A slightly technical, but very readable, series of chapters on all aspects of ocean science written by active research scientists, mostly on the staff of Britain's main oceanographic research institute, and produced to mark the laboratory's move to a major new facility in Southampton.

INDEX

Please note: numbers refer to questions, not pages.